Healthy Churches, Faithful Pastors

Healthy Churches, Faithful Pastors

COVENANT EXPECTATIONS FOR THRIVING TOGETHER

DAVID KECK

An Alban Institute Book

ROWMAN & LITTLEFIELD
Lanham • Boulder • New York • London

Published by Rowman & Littlefield
A wholly owned subsidiary of The Rowman & Littlefield Publishing Group, Inc.
4501 Forbes Boulevard, Suite 200, Lanham, Maryland 20706
www.rowman.com

16 Carlisle Street, London W1D 3BT, United Kingdom

British Library Cataloguing in Publication Information Available

Library of Congress Cataloging-in-Publication Data

Keck, David, 1965–
  Healthy churches, faithful pastors : covenant expectations for thriving together / David Keck.
    pages cm
  Includes bibliographical references.
  ISBN 978-1-56699-755-3 (cloth) — ISBN 978-1-56699-440-8 (pbk.) — ISBN 978-1-56699-450-7 (ebook) 1. Church. 2. Pastoral theology. I. Title.
  BV600.3.K435 2014
  253—dc23   2013018360

∞™ The paper used in this publication meets the minimum requirements of American National Standard for Information Sciences—Permanence of Paper for Printed Library Materials, ANSI/NISO Z39.48-1992.

Printed in the United States of America

Table of Contents

Foreword

Recent studies of congregations have highlighted the relationship of pastors and their churches as crucial to the health of the congregation and the satisfaction of the pastor. Everyone has a horror story to share, but behind the anecdotes and advice circulating at clergy conferences and lay retreats, one discovers two separate conversations sealed off from each other. One is told by pastors, the other by the members of their congregations. This book, by the pastor and scholar David Keck, will help join the two conversations and make them one.

As a pastor, missionary, and former seminary professor, David Keck is ideally suited to facilitate the conversation. That his current congregation (Presbyterian) is situated in the middle of a college campus adds to the richness and complexity of his insights. Keck also holds a PhD in history and has published widely in the field. What he offers to his readers is not advice or war stories. Someone with his experience has certainly earned the right to say, "Let me tell you how it is (was) in my ministry." But he will not do that, for he brings to this book not only his own experience but also a methodological rationale that allows him to do more than extrapolate from his own stories.

In preparation for this book, he interviewed pastors, judicatory officials, and laypeople in a variety of settings. He collated their responses and in several chapters helpfully generalizes his findings by creating six composite characters and allowing them to speak directly to the reader. In the central section of the book, we hear the considered wisdom of the six: a pharmacist, bishop, spiritual director, businessman, senior pastor, and young pastor. The author is a methodologically astute parish pastor whose perspective on research is a bit different than that of a sociologist or a church bureaucrat, both of whom may find themselves distanced from the daily, theological concerns of ministry

David Keck and I enjoyed a collegial relationship at Duke Divinity School, where he translated lived ministry into compelling classroom teaching for mostly untried students. In the classroom, as in this book (and, I suspect, in all his teaching opportunities), he communicates a great deal more than vital data. He also communicates pastoral integrity—his own and that of the office of ministry itself.

This book is designed to create a single, responsible conversation on the pastor-congregation relationship. Keck rightly identifies *expectations* as the key issue.

In seminary, the student may embrace an idealized view of the church as a body of believers eagerly waiting to be led in new and exciting directions. In seminary, "church" is an orderly enterprise in which theology happens on Tuesdays and Thursdays and administration on Wednesdays and Fridays. But in the real church everything happens at once, and expectations of order are often tossed out the window. Younger ministers, who may have tended to overestimate the impact of personality on pastoral effectiveness, might find themselves overwhelmed by the sheer number of things to be done. The title of John Snow's fine book on ministry rings true: *The Impossible Vocation.*

The congregation is a bundle of expectations, too, far more diverse in nature and often more rigid than the pastor's. The "establishment" folks want the congregation to continue as it has always been. Those policies and practices that have sustained the congregation over the years must not change. Representatives of this line of thought should not be dismissed as overly cautious or controlling. The maintenance of ministry—the conduct of services, baptism of babies, instruction of the young, burial of the dead—is no small thing; it represents the presence of God in the human and ecclesial life cycle. Others in the congregation want change. They have seen the future, and they know that a congregation without a mission is a congregation that will die. Still others are sick of programmatic fixes altogether and want genuine instruction in prayer and the spiritual arts. Some of these conflicted expectations have echoed through the congregation from one decade to the next. They were voiced when the last pastor was chosen—and finally left. Old feuds gather steam during a vacancy; grievances are nurtured; positions harden. The pastor, since he or she represents the designated leadership of the entire congregation, can easily become the focus of a series of proxy wars within the congregation.

The title *Healthy Churches, Faithful Pastors* might easily be reversed. Congregations need to get over their internal tensions and renew a vision of corporate faithfulness; pastors who obsess about their own faithfulness, especially if their definition of faithfulness entails doing everything and pleasing everybody, will not be healthy people. Similarly, those who have never learned that ministry is a *disciplined* form of service will confuse laziness with the freedom of the office. The minister's calling is easily fragmented into people-pleasing, nonessential obligations with never enough time to carry them out. Lutheran ethicist and preacher Joseph Sittler described this phenomenon as the "maceration of the minister," a slow but relentless process in which the centrality of the gospel in the minister's life is sliced, diced, and cubed into "contacts" and "units" of effectiveness. The only areas of "give" in the pastoral schedule turn out to be the pastor's self-nurture in the form of study and spiritual development and, as always, his or her family responsibilities.

Here I think Keck's contribution is most important. His book is an instrument for clergy and lay to examine their expectations together, talk about them, and forge realistic expectations in ministry. The book is formatted to facilitate discussion; I read it also as the facilitator of reconciliation.

Even more important, *Healthy Churches, Faithful Pastors* confers theological integrity on the task of clergy-lay dialogue. Keck proposes a covenantal conversation that models itself on God's covenant with Israel and with the church in Jesus Christ. It weighs the theological significance of ordination while recognizing the slippage the ordained office has suffered in recent decades. What does it mean to be ordained? How is ordination a gift from the Holy Spirit? Must its exercise be hierarchical? Keck understands that such questions can only be answered dialogically. He recognizes the mutuality of ministry and understands the congregation as the people of God in mission. Unlike so many studies of congregations, this one does not designate worship as one measure among many of a congregation's effectiveness. Rather, worship belongs to the essence of church. Because we are creatures of God, it is what we do. Chapters in this stimulating book end, fittingly, with "Questions for You and Your Church."

Let the conversation—and the questions—begin.

Richard Lischer
Duke Divinity School

Preface

This book emerged from conversations and is intended to prompt conversations. It is filled with the insights of many people who have shared their experiences and reflections.

I would like to thank all the lay leaders and pastors who have spoken with me in formal and informal ways, in coffee shops, committee meetings, and classrooms, about what went well in their churches and what they regretted. Some of these conversations were delightful; others were melancholy. I am grateful that these men and women were willing to speak from their hearts about important matters affecting congregations and pastors.

In the text, particularly in the epigraphs, they appear as a "Lutheran pastor" or "a Baptist layperson." I have not "named names," not by codified agreement, but as a matter of courtesy. People were glad to talk; whether they were credited or not was largely irrelevant. They simply wanted to share their stories and make a difference, and I am grateful for them. Without their hope-filled desire to improve the relationships between congregations and pastors, this book would have been impossible. The endnotes distinguish between an "interview" and a "conversation." This serves as a reminder that the research for this book took several different forms, and that laypeople and clergy often had something important to say even if they were not being "interviewed."

I am grateful, too, for the support of the Louisville Institute, particularly Sheldon Sorge and Jim Lewis. The research for this book would never have been possible without their grant supporting my project, "How Congregations Can Nurture the Well-Lived Pastoral Life."[1] The Institute respected the symbiotic ideal of the covenant between pastors and congregations, and provided not only financial support for research but also thoughtful guidance in the development of the project. I was fortunate to have several advisors whose insights helped guide my inquiries, and I am thankful for the contributions of Richard Burnett, Keith Meador, Valerie Melvin, Clay Schmit, Therese Schroeder-Sheker, Karen B. Westerfield Tucker, Joanna Walsh, FCJ, and William H. Willimon.

I have very much enjoyed the collaborative work with my editors at the Alban Institute, Beth Anne Gaede, Andrea Lee, and Doug Davidson. This book has an unusual format that is designed to facilitate its use in congregations. This would not have been possible without their careful reading and willingness to explore various possibilities.

This has been a collegial effort, and I am grateful for my colleagues on the Committees of Ministry in New Hope Presbytery and the Presbytery of the Peaks. So, too, am I very, very appreciative of the many people I was privileged to work with at Duke Divinity School, especially Aly Breisch, Nathan Kirkpatrik, Richard Lischer, Sarah Musser, Anne Packett, and Robin Swift. The Divinity School's Clergy Health Initiative allowed me to examine the typescripts of several of its 2008 focus group interviews; the recorded comments from these focus groups provided rich insights for understanding the challenges and joys of pastors.[2]

A number of people have helped in the collation of research and preparation of the manuscript. Many thanks are due to Dianne Hood, Krissy Vick, Shanna Agee, and William Henry.

A (Curious) Note on Surveys

I would also like to thank the many people who responded to various surveys I distributed through denominational sources. Interestingly, I am obliged not to name these judicatories. While some denominational leaders were glad to help, others were cautious. Some leaders were reluctant to have their name or the name of their judicatory be associated with research on how pastors and congregations are or are not thriving together. Therefore, when quotations from surveys are used in the book, the endnotes refer to "author's survey" and provide the date of the particular survey.

I find the reluctance of some denominational officials to be cited in the book to be curious, because I found that individuals were generally welcoming of the opportunity to discuss these matters. They had stories to tell and voices eager to be heard. But somehow, sometimes, we do sadly find ourselves in cautious church structures that discourage open conversation. I trust that God will be with you and your church and will grant you the gifts of hope and courage as you discuss important matters.

Thus, finally, thanks are due to you, too, for your willingness to explore your own community's relationship between pastor(s) and congregation. While there will be reasons for thanksgiving, this is not always an easy task. May God's Spirit continue to bless you abundantly and grant you all you need.

Introduction

WHAT EVERYONE WANTS—A HEALTHY, VIBRANT CHURCH COMMUNITY

Who This Book is For

This book is for congregations and pastors who want to thrive together and who recognize they could use a little help. This book was written for people who want to learn how to improve their church communities, and it comes from fellow Christians who have learned from their own successes and failures and have something to offer.

This book is not about increasing membership rolls or about transforming a church into something new and different (though these may happen in the process). This book is about helping your church do its best as you live out your own identity. This book trusts that God is already at work in the life of your congregation and that most church leaders are already working hard in the service of the church.

Based on my interviews with many pastors and laypeople, as well my reading through research on the dynamics of church life, I have concluded that many of the most common difficulties in churches arise from congregation members and their leaders failing to discuss priorities and expectations and from not finding ways to work through the problems that arise when expectations aren't met. As one pastor reported, "The biggest killer in churches is unrealistic expectations, when people are expecting very different things from each other."[1] For pastors and congregants to arrive at common expectations, they need to understand each other—their respective needs, hopes, and distinctive callings.

Thus, this book is about helping congregants and pastors name the expectations they have for each other. More than fifty "expectation statements" are discussed in chapters 3–10, and they are offered not as a final or exhaustive list but as a starting point for conversations in churches. When people can agree on what they are trying to do together and how they are going to do it, they are able to support one another and flourish. And helping congregations and pastors thrive together is the goal of this book.[2]

How This Book Came to Be

This book began by asking pastors a simple question: "What do you need from your congregants in order for them to help you be a better pastor?"

I had become concerned about relationships between pastors and congregations from my own experiences serving churches, from many conversations with colleagues, from teaching at Duke Divinity School, and from serving on my presbytery's committee that oversees ministers and churches. Why did some people speak of wonderful relationships, while other pastors and laypeople told horror stories? I am grateful that the Louisville Institute recognized the need for further investigation and funded my research project, "How Congregations Can Nurture the Well-Lived Pastoral Life." That support allowed me to continue asking pastors what they needed from their congregations in order to become better pastors.

In response to my question, one pastor looked me in the eye and replied bluntly, "For the church to be the church."[3] Her succinct statement summarized what her colleagues were saying. They expressed this common need in many different ways, of course. Whether speaking gratefully or out of frustration or somewhere in between, pastors identified things such as deeper prayer lives, commitment to church ministries, handling conflict as Christians, or faithful stewardship as what they needed most from congregants. Despite the diversity of such responses, however, pastors said the most fundamental need was for their church members to be the Christians they are called to be. They need the church to be the church.

Pastors were simply describing what most people expect from their church—that it will be a community that enjoys worshipping together, doing things together, and serving others in response to God's love. Whether we are aware of it or not, we expect the church to be a special place that brings out the best in people through the power of God. And this special place is so important because so much of life seems controlled by selfishness, conflict, resentment, or anxiety. The pastors I interviewed simply wanted to help people be part of such a wonderful community. They were speaking not of perfection but of a special place where people are able to enjoy the divine blessings of love, forgiveness, friendship, and helping others.

As the research evolved, and as I realized that pastors also wanted—and needed—to learn from congregants about their expectations for pastors, I asked both pastors and laypeople further questions to explore more details: How can congregants work with their pastors so everyone enjoys being the church together? What gets in the way of good relationships? What simple steps can pastors and congregants take that will make a difference? I listened to Christians share their experiences of healthy and not-so-healthy pastors and churches. I listened to stories that broke my heart and stories that made my eyes water with a hopeful joy. I conducted surveys and read memoirs. Through all these things I discovered some common themes. Here is what folks said:

- Everyone wants the same thing—to thrive together in healthy, mutually beneficial relationships that allow the whole church community to flourish.
- Pastors love their people and have high hopes for them, even when things are challenging. One frustrated pastor, with tears in his eyes, said, "I just wish they knew how much I love them. I want the best for them. Why can't they see that?"[4]
- The laity in the church make all the difference. Effective lay leaders cultivate good pastors and healthy congregations.
- Effective pastoral service depends on the pastor's spiritual, emotional, social, financial, and physical health. Factors that weaken these threaten the entire church's welfare.
- The relationship between pastors and their congregations touches on all aspects of a church's life. If this relationship is strong and vital, the church can be a great place. If it is not, the church can be a terrible emotional (and financial) drain.

Like marriage, a healthy pastorate depends on both sides working on the relationship. (Note that a theme of this book is that pastorates, just like marriages, are best viewed as covenantal relationships rather than contractual relationships; see chapter 1.) Why do so many pastors and churches have difficulty thriving together? Here is what laypeople and pastors shared with me in the hope that their experiences might help others.

- Pastors want to be good pastors, but they often do not ask for the help they need.
- Some pastors are (or become) emotionally unhealthy, and ministry becomes about meeting their own personal needs, not about God's call for the congregation.
- Many pastors are suffering from burnout or heartbreak. They are "getting by" but not thriving. Consequently, their churches are suffering.
- A healthy relationship frequently depends on whether a pastor and a congregation are a good "match" in terms of leadership style or theology—but often people don't know how to detect or address this until it is too late.
- The culture of some churches is welcoming of pastoral leadership, while other churches are hesitant or even mistrustful of their pastors.
- Most congregants want to support their pastor but often don't know how.
- Many, probably most, congregants have little idea of what it is really like to be a pastor.
- Churches want to support their pastors, but they don't really understand their responsibilities toward them.
- Churches do not always know how to cultivate a pastor, how to develop a good one in the first place, or how to help make a good pastor better.

Because pastors are often reluctant to talk about their own needs, and because congregations often don't know what questions to ask or what to look for, conversations that need to happen in churches frequently aren't happening.

That's where this book comes in.

This is a book from church members and pastors to church members and pastors. In these pages you will find Christians speaking to other Christians, trying to share their wisdom and experiences, their regrets and their hopes. In addition to the six composite voices used within the book, the epigraphs throughout the text are intended to let these many contributors speak for themselves on important matters.

What to Expect from This Book

This book has three primary parts as well as two appendices.

The introduction to part I presents a meditation on the nature of expectations and explains the importance of the expectations pastors and congregations have for each other. The two chapters of part I introduce ten principles and six guides for the entire book. The principles provide the framework for understanding the fifty-six expectations discussed in the book; the guides are to prompt conversation about these expectations among pastors and laypeople.

Chapter 1 discusses ten key principles for healthy relationships between pastors and congregations. These principles emerged as central concerns from Scripture, church tradition, and contemporary writers on church dynamics, as well as from interviews and other research. These ten principles reappear throughout the book. (The expectation statements, in turn, are ways of putting the fundamental principles into practice.) Most of the principles are familiar, but reminders are often needed. It will be important to remember some fundamental things such as what *ordination* is and why there are inevitable tensions between pastors and congregations. (*Ordination: Respect for the "Set Apart"* is one of the ten principles; when the key words of the principles are used in the text, they will be in *italics*.)

Chapter 2 presents six composite figures—six fictional men and women imagined from the voices of the many real pastors and laypeople who have contributed to this book. Because these diverse people were influenced by contemporary Christian writers, these composite voices also incorporate the insights of some of the most helpful writers on contemporary church life. As they offer their comments throughout chapters 3–10, they speak honestly—just as the people who spoke with me did. They may remind you of people in your congregation!

Part II focuses on "What Healthy Churches Expect from Faithful Pastors." It begins with a description of what it's like to be a pastor. If this book does nothing else, it will be a success if it gives congregations a better sense of what being a pastor is like. Chapters 3–5, the body of part II, use two-page discussions of specific expectations: specific qualities, practices, or commitments that churches appropriately can expect to see in their pastors.

Part III presents "What Faithful Pastors Expect from Healthy Churches." Chapters 6–10 will follow the same two-page format used in part II, but in these chapters the focus will be on pastors' expectations of their congregation.

Shared expectations for pastors and churches are crucial to building healthy relationships; without agreement on such basic standards, misunderstandings, frustrations, and even anger are likely. To what degree is each of these expectations being met in your church? As you will see, the composite figures have something to say about each expectation. You may disagree with some of the comments or arguments, but you may want to ask yourself if the ideas might be helpful for you and your church.

As the titles of parts II and III suggest, this book strives to encourage *healthy* churches and *faithful* pastors. Of course, it is also essential for pastors to be healthy and churches to be faithful. But the chief problem facing pastors is often being faithful to their calling from God. Pastors let themselves get in the way all too easily—either their own emotional needs, their need to control things, or their inability to get beyond "their" ministry. For their part, the chief challenge facing churches is being a healthy community where a commitment to a greater good allows people to focus on what's truly important. Emotional needs and deep-seated fears, often unstated and therefore surprisingly powerful, are always going to be present, but do they dominate the congregation and make it unhealthy? The New Testament Greek word *sozo* encompasses both "health" and "salvation"—a healthy church can indeed be a place of salvation for everyone.

Finally, the book includes two appendices. The first appendix describes a useful process called a Mutual Ministry Review that allows congregations and pastors to assess how they are doing. Many churches are using such a process to help them develop a shared understanding of how they are to live out the call God has given them. So that readers will have an overview of all the expectations in the book, the second appendix lists them all together in one place, along with the ten principles for a vibrant church community.

How to Use This Book in a Congregation

This book encourages church relationships to be grounded in a *covenant* of mutual respect and welfare (see chapter 1). Therefore, this book should be read together with others. Ideally, pastors and laypeople in congregations would covenant to read it together, perhaps as part of the work of a church council, board, or committee. Some pastors may have a hard time initiating these conversations in their own churches, so they might choose to read it with other pastors. Sunday school classes might want to choose one or more chapters to focus on for a month. There will also be situations where one person in a church will read it by herself, and will find here ways of influencing her church by promoting healthy discussions about shared expectations.

At the beginning of each chapter, the expectation statements are numbered for ease of reference. Each statement is then presented in a two-page spread. If you need to photocopy pages of a few expectation statements for discussions in a church, please do so. But also note that part of the covenant between readers, writers, and publishers is that those who benefit from the work should also purchase the books!

As indicated above, several of the six composite figures will be providing comments and insights on each expectation, and good conversations may be had among readers as they agree or disagree with these guides. One advantage of these fictional characters is that it may be easier to argue with Ed or Lisa than it is to argue with someone in your own church.

At the end of each expectation, there are two scales you can use for prompting meaningful discussions and assessing how your own church is doing with that expectation:

At my church, this Expectation is:

__**Not** Discussed   __**Not** Practiced
__**Not Widely** Agreed Upon   __**Not Widely** Practiced
__**Somewhat** Agreed Upon   __**Somewhat** Practiced
__**Widely** Agreed Upon   __**Widely** Practiced
__**Not** Applicable   __**Not** Applicable

Note that these informal scales invite reflection and conversation about both expressed agreement and actual practice. As you read the book with others in your church, it will be interesting to see if people agree on whether people agree about an expectation! Might further conversations be in order if there is not agreement on agreement? Practice, too, is important—everyone may have a shared expectation, but do people abide by what they've agreed upon? Note that a church could very well practice an expectation without ever actually discussing it. (In such situations it is helpful to remind one another that there is indeed a shared expectation, lest it be neglected over time.) And it might be worth giving special attention to areas where the perspective of the pastor(s) seems markedly different from that of most members of the congregation. Lay leaders may believe there is a consensus in the church on an expectation or that it is being practiced, but the pastor(s) might feel otherwise; such divergences are terrific opportunities for meaningful, productive dialogue.

In order to help prompt conversations, the end of each chapter has questions for discussion. Like the guides and scales, these questions are intended to facilitate thoughtful explorations of the strengths and weaknesses of your church community.

As you engage in these discussions, consider keeping your mind on two questions:

- What can we do now to make a difference?
- What will take more time and effort because it presents some real challenges?

Making forward progress by taking some steps together will be a great blessing. It is easy to let the recognition of a difficult issue paralyze a community. But when people sense good progress, they can approach greater challenges with trust and hope. And purposeful, productive conversations by people who trust in God and one another nurture vibrant churches—churches where God is glorified and the congregation knows joy, peace, and hope.

Although there are significant differences between denominations with regard to church governance and the challenges or opportunities different structures present for pastors and congregations, the interviews conducted for this book revealed many more common dynamics. Similarly, while there are differences between solo pastorates and churches with multiple pastors, people from churches of all sizes expressed similar concerns in interviews and surveys. My hope in writing this book is that you and your church, both pastors and laity—regardless of your denomination or size—will be able to read this book together, assess your own situation, go through the discussion questions at the end of chapters, and make progress in thriving together.

Ultimately, the theme of this book is the *covenant* God ordains between pastors and congregations. God calls a healthy church to sustain a faithful pastor, and God calls a faithful pastor to sustain a healthy church. "For the church to be the church!" That's what pastors need from their congregations—and what congregations need from their pastors. We are called to show in our relationships with one another and in our service to others beyond the church walls that the promise of the gospel and the power of the Spirit are real. We are to strive to be a place where faith and love help instill hope and joy. We are to be a place where we don't have to be afraid, a place where we can have honest disagreements, a place where our best selves can shine forth. In order for the church to be the church, we all need help, encouragement, and mutual *accountability*. It is all too easy to slip into unreflective patterns of avoidance or denial. I trust that the Spirit will use this book to help pastors and laypeople continue to live into the great promise that with God's help we can indeed be God's church. That, after all, is God's *covenant* with all of us.

Part I
Shared Expectations

Introduction
THE POWER OF EXPECTATIONS

A few illustrations of the power of expectations:

- A company has a very profitable quarter, but because it did not meet the market's expectations, its stock decreases in value.
- An athlete frowns as the crowd applauds a fine performance—although the crowd is pleased, she had higher expectations for herself.
- A young married couple runs into difficulties because one spouse expects them both to adhere to a fixed budget while the other prefers to be more flexible.
- A pastor tells herself she should be grateful for her church, but deep down she bears an unconscious grudge against her congregation because she expects to be paid more.
- A politician's campaign team seeks to lower expectations about the results of an election in order to reduce disappointment if things go poorly or to increase excitement if the vote goes well.
- A man retires from a successful business career, but the feeling that he did not live up to his father's expectations continues to nag him.
- A team expects to win a tough game, and they play their best.
- A pastor is frustrated with his new church because he expected members would be more active in leadership roles.
- A congregant of a small church expects his new pastor to be more interested in advancing her career than in building the church, so he perceives the pastor's attempts to launch a new program as an effort to use the church to make a name for herself.
- A church member leaves the church because he expects to be consulted about decisions regarding the church's property, even though he is no longer on the property committee.
- A pastor expects a good response to her sermon, so she preaches with more confidence.

As these examples suggest, our expectations powerfully shape our interactions with others. They shape how we perceive, how we experience, and how we respond. They can even seem to have the force of law. In some cases, to say "I expect you to . . ." really means "Thou shalt . . ." A mediator I spoke with for this project noted that, at its root, disappointment comes when our expectations are not met, and anger arises when our expectations are violated.

Psychologists speak of "confirmation bias"—people tend to see what they expect to see. Hence, expectations and prejudices can be deeply related. ("Prejudice," or pre-judging, is a form of "expecting.") For example, a young black man simply walking down the street might be viewed with suspicion because stereotypes cause some to expect him to be a criminal.

The placebo effect in medicine likewise demonstrates the power of expectations. A sugar pill can make us healthier if we believe it is a genuine drug, and we expect it to make us better. Expectations shape health.

Music depends on expectations. Listeners come to anticipate that a phrase or chord will move in a certain direction, so skilled composers learn how both to meet these expectations and to play off of people's expectations to create delightful surprises.

Expectations also shape self-esteem and interpersonal outcomes. As people in sales and marketing will remind us, if a person expects a "yes," she is much more likely to get a sale.

Expectations can also function as a kind of "entitlement"—we expect something so strongly that we assume it is our just due—and, rightly or wrongly, we grow upset if expectations are not met.

So powerful is the language of expectation that since the early nineteenth century a pregnant woman has been said to be "expecting." Expecting—preparing to bring life into the world.

In Matthew 24 and 25, Jesus calls upon his followers to be awake and ready for—to expect—the return of the Son of Man. And those who would follow him are also expected to discern the presence of Jesus in the "least of these" (Matthew 25:40). Christians are to be an expecting people, people on the lookout for God and God's kingdom.[1] Theologically, expectation is one aspect of our Christian hope, and by faith we hold that our expectations of God are trustworthy. And note that Christians differ from one another in this regard. One person may expect a prayer to be answered, whereas another feels she is hoping beyond hope for an answer. Both are faithful, but their estimations of what God is likely to do have been shaped differently.

We form our expectations in diverse ways. (In order to do justice to the sometimes-mysterious way in which expectations develop, we might say that expectations "arise" or "emerge.") Often expectations are deeply rooted in our understanding of God, the world, and ourselves. They come from experiences in families, schools, culture, churches, Bible studies, and shopping malls. They emerge over time as we observe and imitate norms, patterns, and habits of behavior. Our expectations can be healthy, delusional, or even pathological.

Some expectations are the result of explicit statements or directives. A coach may make it perfectly clear that he expects team members to be on time for practice—and he may be perfectly willing to mete out consequences to those who don't live up to his expectations. This kind of clarity makes it easier for everyone to function together as a team. Everyone in the group is consciously aware of common standards for behavior, and they understand that they can be held accountable.

Other expectations develop unconsciously from cultural norms, social patterns, and our personalities. And they can be incredible powerful precisely because they often arise without our being aware of them.

In some cultures it is expected that polite guests will leave a little food on their dinner plates as a sign that the host has provided more than enough. But in other societies, the polite thing to do is to eat all the food to demonstrate that the host has provided a delicious meal. By violating unstated expectations, a guest can be rude quite unintentionally.

Similarly, someone who grows up in a home with boisterous family dinners where parents and children vigorously disagree on all kinds of things is likely to have different expectations for how people should behave in committees than someone whose family dinners were quiet times. These two committee members have probably never discussed what's appropriate for conversations, but it is likely that one expects interruptions while the other finds them problematic and possibly threatening.

When people speak of optimists or pessimists, they are noticing that some people tend to expect good outcomes and others expect something bad will happen. Our experiences of events reinforce such personality tendencies. The optimist expects a good outcome, and "sees" something different from the pessimist. The optimist thus is confirmed in his optimism (just as the pessimist experiencing the same event might be confirmed in his pessimism—after all, the glass *is* half-empty). Thus, what is realistic to one person might be unrealistic to another depending on each person's sense of what is likely or possible.

For all their immense power to shape perception and responses, expectations can also be changed as people discuss what should be considered appropriate or faithful. This book intends to facilitate this process in churches because agreed-upon expectations are one of the central ingredients for thriving in community life. As the initial examples might well suggest, pastors who have unrealistic or inappropriate expectations of themselves and their congregations are likely to become sadly disappointed or even angry. And congregations that have unstated, unrealistic, or inappropriate expectations of both themselves and their pastors are likely to become frustrated or fall into conflict.

Yet how often do churches discuss fundamental expectations about responsibilities, behavior, and goals? The self-assessment response scale for use with the expectation statements in chapters 3–10 includes a "not discussed much" option precisely because my research leads me to believe most churches have not discussed many of these expectations. These expectations themselves emerged as the shared wisdom of multiple sources, including Scripture, church tradition, interviews, contemporary authors, and surveys. Congregations and pastors that can discuss these and put as many of them as possible into practice will discover the joys of thriving together in a *covenant*. Meeting these expectations is not something pastors and congregations have *got to do*. Rather, living into such expectations is something congregations and pastors *get to do*—for their *covenant* is called into being and sustained by the power of the living God.

Part I of this book lays the foundation for discussing these expectations in churches. Chapter 1 presents "Ten Principles for a Vibrant Church Community," principles that already may be at work consciously or unconsciously in many people's expectations for relationships between pastors and congregations. In order for communities to agree on what is expected, they need to have some fundamental principles in place. Principles govern expectations, and expectations are powerful in part because they guide the way people actually live out their core values.

Chapter 2 offers "Six Guides for You and You Church," six composite characters who have various perspectives on churches and what Christians should expect from one another. Throughout chapters 3–10, these individuals will offer advice and comments on each expectation. These composite characters represent the real voices of diverse laypeople and pastors I interviewed for this book. You are invited to agree or disagree with them and their various approaches to church life. Considering how you might respond to Ed may help you think about how you might react to a person in your congregation who thinks much like Ed but also sings in the choir with you.

Hearing these composite voices sharing their expectations may help people in churches to share their own expectations—and this is often not an easy task. Because, as noted above, "I expect . . ." can sound like "Thou shalt . . ." Christians may be concerned about imposing their will on others. We sometimes prefer silence to appearing too forward or too needy. But often the greatest gift we can give in a relationship, a group, or a church is a clear statement of our own hopes, principles, and expectations. How else will those who love us know how to love us?

1

Ten Principles for a Vibrant Church Community

Purpose: Striving to Be the Church
Ordination: Respect for the "Set Apart"
Covenant: A Life-Giving Relationship
Mutual Ministry: We All Serve Together
Resurrection: "Practice Resurrection"
Eustress: Keeping the Inevitable Tensions in Tune
Safety: Don't Take It for Granted
Maturity: Cultivating Honesty, Trust, and Self-Knowledge
Accountability: The Sacrament of Failure
Boundaries: The Difference between Bad and Good, Good and Great

The ten principles for a vibrant church community detailed in this chapter describe virtues and practices that are foundational for exploring how pastors and congregations can thrive together.

Some of them may seem obvious. A church with a strong sense of *mutual ministry* and ingrained habits of practicing *accountability* with steadfast love is likely to be a place where people enjoy coming together to worship God and serve God's kingdom. I've learned, however, not to take any of these principles for granted. If a church community lacks one or more of these, there are almost certainly some fundamental problems. If there is no shared sense of *purpose*, there is no real community. If *maturity* is lacking, particularly in a pastor, everyone suffers. If the pastor does not have a sense of *safety* as a servant-leader in a particular church, then he is neither leading nor serving.

These principles emerged from four sources—the Bible, church tradition, contemporary writers on church life, and interviews conducted for this book. Scripture contains abiding organizational wisdom as well as revelations about the nature and character of God. Scholars over the last several decades have studied U.S. churches and discerned essential characteristics of healthy relationships between pastors and congregations. And, significantly, the laypeople and pastors I spoke with identified the same basic set of values that Scripture and contemporary scholarship identified. To be sure, some might choose other terms for inclusion in this list of principles (such as generosity or hospitality). But these ten speak to the heart of the relationship between congregations and pastors, and they are broad enough to include other virtues. (Generosity, for example, is one aspect of a *covenant.*)

Chapters 3–10 present expectation statements for pastors and congregations to discuss and—hopefully—agree upon. If these expectations are the "meat" of the book (the muscle and vital organs), the following ten principles are the indispensable bones that support the body and give it a sturdy structure. A broken bone may require the rest of the body to make awkward, compensating adjustments, but a healthy skeletal foundation helps the rest of the body to thrive.

Purpose: Striving to Be the Church

In his classic *Man's Search for Meaning,* psychiatrist and concentration-camp survivor Viktor E. Frankl explores the importance of individuals and communities having meaning in their lives. Having meaning, having a reason to live, allows people to endure great difficulties and indeed to experience abiding joy.[1] Not surprisingly, when asked what they need from their congregations in order to thrive, pastors spoke about having meaning, a reason for their service. Put most generally, pastors stated that what they most needed was for the members of their congregations to work together as they all strive to be a church community with meaning, a church perhaps that in its own way takes up Jesus' Great Commission: "Go therefore and make disciples of all nations, baptizing them in the name of the Father and of the Son and of the Holy Spirit, and teaching them to obey everything that I have commanded you" (Matthew 28:19–20).

A pastor flourishes when she can see that her work is making a difference, that her congregation is indeed embracing this Great Commission (or some other expression of Christian *purpose*) by seeking to live according to the Bible and their denomination's teachings. The Constitution of the Presbyterian Church (USA) suggests what this might look like with its naming of the great ends of the church:

> The great ends of the church are the proclamation of the gospel for the salvation of humankind; the shelter, nurture, and spiritual fellowship of the children of God; the maintenance of divine worship; the preservation of the truth; the promotion of social righteousness; and the exhibition of the Kingdom of Heaven to the world.[2]

Significantly, the mission of the church is more important than institutional survival: the church is to bear witness to Christ "even at the risk of losing its life." There are many different ways of living out these great ends faithfully, and each congregation and each pastor will do this in a distinctive manner. People of good faith will disagree on mission priorities; that is a sign of the diverse ways God chooses to work in the world. (When a pastor's priorities match well with the congregation's, we often say there is a "good fit" between pastor and congregation.) Regardless of a congregation's specific identity and priorities, the essential characteristic remains having meaning.

The word *purpose* sums up the importance of meaning-filled Christian striving for such great ends of the church. *Purpose* is another way of asking, "Why are we here?" And as the plural "great ends" suggest, a congregation's primary *purpose* will most likely include many smaller purposes—numerous important activities that together make up a larger identity.

Healthy, meaning-filled churches have identities and roles in their communities. They have a sense that they are sharing in something larger than themselves—indeed, that they are responsible stewards of their own corner of the kingdom of God. Through their experience of working hard together on challenging tasks, they come to know the power of God. Whether they have a formal mission statement or not, every member of a healthy congregation trusts that they have a common *purpose* that brings out the best in them. Such congregations are indeed clear about why they have a pastor in the first place; they recognize the significance of pastor Robert H. Ramey's subtitle to his book on pastors and congregations: *Fulfilling God's Mission*.[3]

By contrast, as one denominational executive noted in her conversation with me, unhealthy churches lack a common *purpose*. She had worked with congregations that once had a shared sense of mission but, over the years, gradually lost a sense of the importance of this mission. As a consequence, these churches tended to focus on the individual needs of their members. They came to lack clarity about organization and funding priorities. Many got by, but they didn't thrive anymore.[4]

Faithful pastors serve in churches because God calls them to that *purpose*. (The next principle, *ordination*, underscores God's work in pastoral leadership.) But some pastors serve churches for unhealthy reasons or other purposes (hence the emphasis on *maturity* and *boundaries*). Some congregations may need to help their pastors realize this unpleasant fact (hence the importance of *accountability*). Yet, as the success of pastor and author Rick Warren's book, *The Purpose-Driven Life,* suggests, discerning God's *purpose* for a person and a community is profoundly inspiring.

Ordination: Respect for the "Set Apart"

To be ordained means to be set apart for God's *purposes*. In Romans 1:1, Paul declares that he has been "set apart *for* the gospel of God." And in Acts 13:2, the Holy Spirit tells the church to "set apart" Paul and Barnabas "*for* the work to which I have called them" (italics added). The word translated as "set apart" means literally "to sever," and the Bible provides many examples of those separated out of the community for the sake of serving God and the community—including priests, Levites, deacons, bishops, and elders. Today, denominational formulations vary, but most ordination vows ask a great deal from the persons taking them. These vows, which describe God's expectations for God's pastors and other ordained church officers, ask these men and women to be different, indeed, to be "set apart." Baptism commissions all Christians to service, but ordination is a special form of commissioning.

Being set apart entails dangers and sacrifices. Many pastors speak of loneliness. Most laypeople are free to choose whichever church they want, but in most traditions, pastors surrender this "right," just as they surrender the capacity to sit next to their spouse and children during worship. It is hardly surprising that most of the biblical stories in which God calls people to serve depict those people as resisting or protesting like Moses or Isaiah, or even trying to get away like Jonah. (People who had a hard time in high school because they were perceived as "different" may be able to empathize with the plight of pastors!)

That some church members have little respect for ordained ministers will hardly be a surprise. Many of us have known people who were suspicious or even hostile to ministers or who simply had no regard for what ministers have to say. In today's culture, respecting the authority of another person does not always come easily. Additionally, some Christians have been badly hurt by a pastor and, therefore, have difficulty sharing in the life of a congregation.

That some pastors show little respect for their own *ordination* may be a bit more surprising. This may reflect an underdeveloped understanding of the depth and breadth of ordained ministry. A pastor may not recognize the seriousness of the calling. (The many biblical passages about God's wrath are a reminder that God is passionately for some things and against others.) A pastor may desire to "fit in" and to be liked, but critical distance from a congregation, as difficult as this is, is required of ordained ministry. The paradox that all pastors live with is that they are the public face of a church while also being called to be set apart from that congregation. They are both at the center and on the outside.

Healthy respect for *ordination*, respecting the life of being "set apart" requires respecting both the office and the person. Both congregations and pastors need to respect the authority vested in the pastor, trusting that he is indeed sent by God to that community. At the same time, every pastor needs to earn respect from a congregation. She does this by respecting her own *ordination*, her calling, and her awareness that she is there on no one's orders but God's.

Like all forms of authority, the authority that comes with ordination can be abused. This book is respectful of that danger; in fact, one goal of this book is helping pastors and congregations come to healthy view of *ordination*. In some cases the pastor will need to help the congregation grow in its understanding. In other cases, the congregation may have to help the pastor be clear about what the expectations of *ordination* are.

Covenant: A Life-Giving Relationship

One of the most important themes in this book is *covenant*. The third of the ten principles involves congregations supporting and working collegially with those "set apart." In a covenantal approach to pastoral relations, a church responds to the fact that the pastor's "set-apartness" (and the difficulties it entails) is for the good of the community.

Covenants within a church are ultimately based on God's covenant with us. In Genesis 17, God covenants with Abraham and his descendants to be their God. Significantly, this covenant and the new covenant of Christ both entail blood, the blood of circumcision and the blood of the cross. This giving of lifeblood reminds us that covenants are powerful and life-giving, and are not to be entered into lightly. This book will develop the importance of *covenant* from a number of different perspectives; in some sense, the whole book is about helping congregations and pastors name the elements of their *covenant* before God and to live out this *covenant* faithfully in their lives together.

What is a *covenant?* It is perhaps easiest to see what a covenant is by seeing how a covenant differs from a contract.

In a contract, two parties agree to exchange goods and services, often for unrelated goals. A contract is negotiated primarily from the perspective of mutual self-interest. The buyer wants ten widgets at the lowest price she can get, and the seller wants to provide the ten widgets at the highest price she can get. The buyer's welfare is not really a concern of the seller (and vice versa), unless the buyer's welfare affects the seller's own welfare. The parties may or may not trust each other; they may even want to know that legal remedies exist in case the other party fails to deliver. The buyer may expect the seller who has promised ten widgets by a specific date to make extraordinary, even potentially self-destructive sacrifices to fulfill the contract. A sure sign of a problem with a congregation's attitude toward its pastor is when members view the pastor as a "hire," someone under contract.

By contrast, in a *covenant,* the two parties are deeply concerned about the welfare of each other. There is trust and shared goals, a common *purpose.* The goods and services provided are important—but they are only a part of the relationship. We think of marriage as a *covenant* precisely because the welfare of one spouse is a primary concern of the other. A faithful spouse does not present demands that will harm the other. (Note that covenanting with a pastor also involves the pastor's family; see *boundaries* below.) *Covenants* bring out the best in us as we come to realize the delights of loving and being loved. We willingly accept sacrifices when necessary because we recognize that covenantal relationships are deeply meaningful and life-giving. Indeed, such sacrifices hardly seem sacrifices at all.

Healthy churches have covenants with their pastors, not contracts. Mutual regard for the other's welfare, not mutual self-interest, is the basis for this relationship. Each side commits to be faithful to the other and to hold each other accountable in love (see *accountability* below) as together they seek to fulfill their common *purpose.* (Like a marriage, a *covenant* between a pastor and a congregation requires ongoing nurture in order to remain strong.) This is the vision underlying Paul's statement in Galatians 6:6: "Those who are taught the word must share in all good things with their teacher." And this sharing in all good things—this profound mutuality grounded in the gospel—can help make possible what pastor and author Richard John Neuhaus described in his evocatively titled book *Freedom for Ministry*.[5]

Mutual Ministry: We All Serve Together

In churches, a *covenant* is for ministry—more specifically, for *mutual ministry*.

The person God sets apart as pastor for a congregation has distinctive responsibilities. Generally, these include preaching the Word, administering the sacraments, providing pastoral care, and working collegially in church governance. Another responsibility of church leadership is helping everyone in the congregation respond to their own call to serve God, their church, and their church's witness in the world. This is the vision of *mutual ministry*.

There are many aspects of ministry, many tasks that need doing, many responsibilities. Who is going to do all these things? More importantly, who *should* be doing all these things? The pastor is not to do all these things by himself. Not only does this lead to pastoral burnout, but it can also interfere with congregants' ability to find meaning and *purpose* in the community. (The story of the origin of the office of deacon in Acts 6 is a reminder that these challenges go back to the earliest years of the church.) Healthy churches provide members opportunities for serving God and others. Think of all the people Paul mentions in his letters who are co-workers with him in so many different ways. In unhealthy churches pastors often do most of the work or are expected to do too much of it. *Mutual ministry* describes the ways in which church members and the pastor(s) serve together, each assuming specific responsibilities.

As noted above under *purpose*, God expects the entire church to bear witness to the Good News of Jesus Christ. Every church member, by virtue of her baptism, is called to some form of ministry in the life of a church. Indeed, the New Testament vision of the church is of the Spirit entrusting diverse gifts to different Christians so the church can thrive in both its common life together and its public witness. God expects—and provides for!—different members of the church community to be teachers, healers, prophets, caregivers, and more. One of the crucial tasks of church leadership, therefore, is to "equip the saints for the work of ministry" (Ephesians 4:12). And the "saints" include everyone in the congregation, not just the pastor or church staff. For a local church to be faithful to God's expectations, the pastor cannot be the only person in ministry in a church. (The powerful phrase "the priesthood of all believers" cherished by many Protestants is a good reminder of God's high calling to all Christians.) *Mutual ministry* is the gospel's inviting everyone to a meaningful, *purpose*-filled life, a life that can make a difference for others.

Sometimes a lack of genuine *mutual ministry* is a failure of the pastor. Being too eager to please or too eager to show he is making a difference in "his" ministry, the pastor takes on too many tasks and does not allow lay leaders to flourish. At other times the problem is with the congregation or lay leadership. Implicitly or explicitly, they prefer paying the pastor to do everything so they don't have to do much themselves.

Because congregations sometimes do not review and articulate their responsibilities, there is often confusion as to roles. As one pastor said, "There are a hundred members in my church, and I have a hundred different job descriptions."[6] How is this person going to know how to prioritize her Friday afternoon? Should she visit a sick parishioner, work on her sermon, gather information for the budget, fix the leaky sink in the church kitchen, write a letter to the newspaper protesting an injustice, or read a book about how pastors and congregations can thrive together? One of the greatest gifts a church can give a pastor is a clear statement of pastoral priorities. If you want your pastor to serve most effectively, your church needs to work with her so she knows (1) what she needs to focus on and (2) what responsibilities others will assume.

The appendix on "Conducting a Mutual Ministry Review" may help with this process. In such a review, the important questions of *What should the pastor be doing?* and *How is the pastor doing?* are set into the context of the broader questions, *What should church members be doing?* and *How are we all doing together in mutual ministry?* Such an approach—which is grounded in the *covenant* between the congregation and the pastor—will encourage everyone to name and celebrate the gifts they have received from God and find ways to share them.

Resurrection: "Practice Resurrection"

Farmer and poet Wendell Berry concludes his poem "Manifesto: The Mad Farmer Liberation Front" with the call to "practice resurrection."[7] Berry's poem is about the freedom and power that can come from trusting the power of the Creator of all things. His urgent advice reminds us that death and resurrection is the central dynamic of the Christian life, a continuing process of dying to the old and living into the new. For pastors and congregations to thrive together, they must be willing to practice resurrection.

Congregations may need to die to their expectations of what a pastor should be. Even a pastor who has been in a church for several years will find that she is still being compared with the previous minister. While inevitable, this is not healthy. Each pastor is unique, and each pastor wants to be respected for who he is. Congregations may also need to let previous habits, practices, and ministries die. One of the great mistakes churches make is failing to see themselves as organisms that face challenges of survival, change, adaptation, and even death. Just because something has always been done a certain way does not mean there is any vitality left in it. If a previous *purpose* no longer energizes and provides joyful meaning, it may be time to discern a new *purpose*.

Pastors, too, need to practice resurrection. I've known many pastors who arrive at a new church still grieving their departure from a previous congregation. That is not fair to the new church. Other pastors may need to let some part of themselves die, perhaps an illusion about who they are or are capable of becoming. Still other pastors need to let some false dreams for a church and their own personal ministries die. This is all part of developing more professional *maturity*.

The principle of *resurrection* reminds us that pastors and congregations must work together in trust and hope as they negotiate the processes of change required of healthy organisms. Indeed, Jesus observes that unless a kernel dies it will not bear new life (John 12:24). It is perfectly okay to let things die, even cherished things, because we trust the Giver of Life is at work in our midst. Despite our worries and doubts, we can take risks in *safety* (see below) because we know God works all things for the good. The good news of the gospel is that cross-bearing leads to *resurrection*.

Resurrection is thus a gesture of letting go—letting go of illusions, false aspirations, long-held notions, long-standing attitudes, or even previous successes. It is a way of being in the world with open hands, hands that are open to receive and share, not hands that are clenched and clinging. *Resurrection* is a kind of generosity of spirit that allows a pastor and congregation to receive one another in love and hope.

Eustress: Keeping the Inevitable Tensions in Tune

The term *eustress* literally means "good stress."

We are accustomed to seeing stress, tension, and conflict in mostly negative terms. But this word, coined by endocrinologist Hans Selye, reminds us not only that tension is inevitable but also that it is a potential source for good.[8] Or—perhaps more accurately—some form of stress is required for the good.

Selye separated "stress" into distress (stress that is harmful) and *eustress*. Overcoming a challenge, physical exercise, giving birth, falling in love, or preaching the gospel—these all involve physical or psychological stress that is well worth it. *Eustress* increases human capacity, achievement, and meaning. If our goal is to avoid all stress, we miss many of life's joys. Similarly, the body itself thrives on tension. Although we associate "tension" with "tension headaches" or "nervous tension," our muscles require tension—more specifically, alternating actions of tension and relaxation. Proper use of tension in exercise leads to muscle tone. Indeed, an organism without stress, tension, and tone is a blob, a formless mass incapable of movement or vitality. (I hope this does not sound like your church!)

Inevitably churches have distinctive, stressful tensions. In *Managing Polarities in Congregations*, authors Roy M. Oswald and Barry Johnson call such tensions "polarities."[9] They characterize polarities as power struggles over opposing views. Both sides have a legitimate point (for example, one person suggests a surprise memorial gift should go to the poor; another believes the church should spend this money to maintain its building). But because of the human tendency to use either/or thinking, conflict develops. The person who feels he is right often believes his opponent must be wrong. But in many situations each side of the argument needs the other for the church to be complete.

These polarities or tensions typically involve two values, priorities, or commitments that are present to some degree in every church. Some tensions are characteristic of the office of pastor: Should the pastor spend more time on visitation or sermon preparation? Should the sermon comfort or challenge the congregation? Does a particular situation call for leading or serving?

Some tensions are characteristic of congregations: Which is more dominant in a congregation—tradition or openness to change? Do we focus on caring for church members or reaching out to the community?

And some are simply inherent in the nature of being Christian and bearing witness to God in the world: Jesus declares that the kingdom of God is already at hand (Mark 1:15). But as we await his return, the horrific accounts that fill each day's newspaper remind us that the kingdom has not yet fully arrived. Christian celebration of the "already" remains in tension with the abiding sorrows of the "not yet." Similarly, as Christians, do we practice forgiveness or accountability? Clearly, as Oswald and Johnson note, both ends of the polarity/tension are important, but we need to understand how to hold the two together faithfully.

Therese Schroeder-Sheker, a harpist and an innovator in the field of end-of-life care, uses the metaphor of tuning the strings of a harp as a way of imagining how we can thrive with tension.[10] Churches are under a tremendous amount of tension. So, too, are harps, and we can learn a great deal about how to be a healthy church from a harp. The musical qualities of the harp depend on:

- a structure that can withstand stress
- an empty soundboard that allows for the resonating of strings in tension to sound forth beautifully
- careful and regular tuning

When a well-made harp is in tune, it is beautiful, splendid, evocative, and healing. But when the strings of the harp are too loose, the harp is flat. And when the strings are too tight, they are sharp—or they snap.

Does your church have a sturdy physical-emotional-spiritual constitution that can withstand stress? Does your church have a soundboard, an inner spaciousness that allows you to work constructively and beautifully with tensions? Or is life in your church filled up with so many agendas and issues that there is no resonate space? And does your church have a healthy way of keeping itself in tune, a life-giving process that allows tensions to be named and used for the good of the kingdom? (See *purpose* above.)

This book seeks to help pastors and congregations find ways to keep the inevitable tensions of church life in tune. As you reflect on these tensions, keep the image of a well-tuned harp in mind. And note that just as a harp may be tuned in several different keys, so there is no single right tuning for a pastor or church. These are worked out individually and may change over time. What begins as a C major tuning in one season of life may well become A major in another. This image of tuning is a way of transforming tension—and even church conflict—into *eustress*.

Healthy churches and healthy pastorates depend to a great extent on how these inevitable tensions and stresses of churches are addressed. The good news is that we do not need to be afraid. How often have we recognized that the right thing to do will be difficult, even stressful, for us and cause us tension? This is *eustress*, and it is essential for congregational vitality.

Safety: Don't Take It for Granted

If people do not feel safe, they cannot thrive.

I remember a church meeting where a retiree expressed his opinions in a loud manner, signaling to everyone that he was determined to have his way. He did not yell or threaten, but after the meeting, another lay leader confided in me and said, "He was just like my father when he used to get mad at us." For her, this meeting was not safe. She was not able to listen, discern, and speak with comfort, and thus her ability to serve faithfully was compromised.

As this example illustrates, *safety* in a congregation is not just physical; it takes many forms. Does the pastor feel safe to be herself, or does she worry about how her love of, say, rock music might be perceived? Do congregants feel comfortable approaching the pastor with doubts about faith or anger with God? Does the pastor hesitate to preach on some parts of the Bible for fear of how the congregation will react? Do members in the church feel safe to express their ideas in public conversations, or do most feel more comfortable talking privately in the parking lot after a meeting?

The question of *safety* requires that we consider the extent to which a congregation is governed by fear or anxiety. These are present in every person and in every community. The question is the extent to which these predominate—or under what circumstances people let fear dominate their actions. Jesus frequently says, "Do not be afraid," and this remains an important message. And 1 John 4:18 offers a beautiful vision of what we can hope for: "There is no fear in love, but perfect love casts out fear."

Safety requires balancing—or finding the right tuning of the tension between—*accountability* and support. (See both *eustress* above and *accountability* below.) *Accountability* checks inappropriate, threatening behavior, but it can be too confrontational and can drive people away. Personal support promotes the sense of welcome that is often required for people to be comfortable in a community—but while all people should be welcome, not all behavior should be accepted. Too much *accountability* or too much support will not provide a safe space. As the saying goes, support without accountability is cheap grace. Accountability without support is cruel.

Maturity: Cultivating Honesty, Trust, and Self-Knowledge

Safety and *maturity* are profoundly related. A congregation of mature adults is able to be a safe place for everyone. A congregation dominated by immature people is a dangerous place, no matter what the church mission statement says. And a safe church can promote the maturation process of its members. It is hardly surprising that several New Testament epistles stress the importance of having emotionally healthy, self-disciplined persons as leaders (see, for example, 1 Timothy 3 and Titus 1).

For the purposes of this book, *maturity* encompasses a number of different qualities and abilities, especially honesty, trustworthiness, and self-knowledge. A mature person is aware of her actions, the underlying causes for her behavior, and the impact she might have on others. She recognizes her freedom and the importance of responsible action. She seeks to bring her actions into line with her ideals, recognizing that she will make mistakes and will need to make amends. The mature person is able to be both deeply connected to others and independent from them. She is able to negotiate tensions and conflict (see *eustress* above) and has respect for the diversity of roles in a community (see *ordination* and *covenant* above). Turning aside from the works of the flesh and empowered by the Spirit, she bears the fruit of the Spirit, including love, peace, gentleness, and self-control (see Galatians 5:19–23).

Maturation is a lifelong process. Indeed, as we proceed through the joy and crises of life, we will face challenges to our identities and our capacities for behaving as responsible adults. Not everyone can thrive soon after a catastrophic event. Not everyone has ways of growing through problems, crises, or chronic stress. Sometimes the imminent death of a loved one makes it very difficult for a person to behave in a mature way.

Both pastors and congregations may need help. Some pastors do not have the inner strength to thrive in some congregations. Sometimes a pastor can get so deeply enmeshed with a congregation that he loses the ability to step back and recognize how his own behavior is restricting the congregation. Or a pastor may become so dependent on positive feedback from the congregation that she has a very hard time with constructive criticism.

Congregations may not be helping their pastors. A lay leader compared churches to homeowners associations: "People know they can't get kicked out, so these are places where they can take out their frustrations or assert their need for control."[11] Church members may be angry about their work, their home life, or their physical health, but since they feel helpless to affect these, they may look for outlets. Immature people are often unable to recognize what motivates them at a given moment. They may claim to be doing something for the good of the church when, in fact, they are working out some other problem in their lives.

Accountability: The Sacrament of Failure

The best way to promote *maturity* is to practice *accountability*. Most parents know this, but some churches don't.

The constitution of the Presbyterian Church (USA) includes a number of confessions that bear witness to its understanding of God, the church, and its mission in the world. One of these describes the signs of the authentic church in terms of "the true preaching of the Word of God . . . the right administration of the sacraments of Christ Jesus . . . and . . . ecclesiastical discipline uprightly ministered as God's Word prescribes."[12]

But people don't like being held accountable (just ask the prophets), nor do they like holding others accountable. Even the word *discipline* sounds unpleasant. But *accountability*, discipline according to God's Word, is required. Indeed, in Hebrews 12, discipline is a sign of God's parental love. Discipline and discipleship share the same root—and they belong together.

As with *eustress* and *safety* above, *accountability* requires faithfully tuning between too little and too much. Some pastors (and church members) are allowed to get away with anything by adoring or deferential congregants. Others don't get any slack at all, and suspicious or hostile church members are more than ready to hold the pastor's feet to the fire. The first of these conditions becomes a license for irresponsible behavior. The second means that pastors—or other members of a church, if they feel targeted—may come to church wary and overly cautious, if not fearful for their *safety*.

How many churches have been weakened by unchecked inappropriate behavior? How many people have been driven from a church by an over-zealous approach to rules? How many pastors feel so pressured to be right all the time that they can't admit a mistake? How many congregants are concerned by a pastor's apparent lack of preparation for worship and yet say nothing about it? How many pastors and lay leaders have failed to speak with a church member about circulating harmful emails or some other form of disrespectful behavior?

Congregations and pastors need to practice *accountability*, forgiveness, and reconciliation in such a way that these become signs of God's grace at work, a kind of sacrament. God expects us to be fruitful, not perfect. And part of the way we become fruitful is by practicing *accountability* in love. Therese Schroeder-Sheker calls this the "Sacrament of Failure"—God's transforming and renewing grace at work in the midst of our weaknesses and mistakes.[13]

If we can trust that we are part of a community committed to the Sacrament of Failure, we are much more likely to be able to admit our mistakes. We can ask for forgiveness and help. We can find ways to make amends. The recognition that we need not live in fear of guilt or shame becomes, then, a sign of grace, a sacrament. *Accountability* thus is no longer about blame or punishment but takes on the liberating quality of *resurrection*.

Indeed, one of the surest signs of a healthy relationship is the ability to be honest with one another, especially when it comes to asking someone to reflect on and even change his or her behavior. More accurately, perhaps, relationships become deeper, more meaningful, and healthier precisely through practicing *accountability*.

Boundaries: The Difference between Bad and Good, Good and Great

Boundaries establish limits. One of the great dangers facing pastors and congregations is that the role of the pastor can be without limits. Most church members expect to have boundaries that separate their personal lives from their professional lives. But as the widow of a pastor noted, "Being a pastor is the one profession where the only boundary is whether people like you."[14]

In an unhealthy church there are few boundaries between pastor and church. Her identity is woven completely with the life of the church, its successes and failures, and her being liked by the congregation. And, for its part, the church feels free to call upon—or check in on—the pastor at any time, for any purpose. One church, which provided a manse (or parsonage) to its pastor, insisted on the right to keep keys to the building and to drop in at any time to make sure "everything was in good working order." Fortunately for this pastor (who was a a single woman), her bishop told her to have the locks changed, send him the bill, and give him the phone number of the appropriate committee member at the church. Other pastors are not so well supported by their denominations. As Duke Divinity School's Clergy Health Initiative demonstrates, poor boundaries lead not only to unhealthy churches but also to unhealthy pastors.[15]

Almost from the beginning of the history of the church, pastoral leaders have struggled with identifying responsibilities and setting *boundaries*. In Acts 6, the early church designates seven individuals to assume some of the duties required of the rapidly expanding church, duties the apostles would otherwise have assumed, thus taking them away from one of their primary responsibilities, the "ministry of the Word." Similarly, in a healthy church, the pastor and congregation have set clear *boundaries*. Expectations about time and roles are clear. *Covenant, mutual ministry, maturity,* and *accountability* are all in evidence. The pastor can be away from the church, and the church has been well prepared to function without the constant presence of the pastor. Emergencies happen, and pastors are called in the middle of the night, but these are viewed as extraordinary circumstances; it is clear the pastor is not at the congregation's beck and call.

A pastoral counselor shared the story of a church where one of the matrons of the congregation expected the pastor to come over to her house every Christmas and help her make a coconut cake. When a new pastor came to the church, he politely refused. Years later, when he was leaving the church on good terms, this woman told him he was the only pastor at that church she'd ever respected. Although he had initially caused her some consternation, she ultimately saw in him someone focused on his distinctive responsibilities as her pastor. A pastor who did not have a good sense of *boundaries* formed by a strong theology of *ordination* might have been tempted to do anything to please the church member, even helping crack coconuts. But, as this story shows, making someone happy is not the same as earning respect.

Based on his experience in working with pastors, this pastoral counselor concluded that boundaries are what "sets a great pastor apart from a good pastor."[16] *Boundaries* promote *mutual ministry* and effective service by the entire church (see *purpose* above). Pastors therefore need to practice good *boundaries*. Or, more accurately, pastors and congregations thrive together when they have the *maturity* to *covenant* together to establish and maintain good *boundaries*.

Boundaries are especially important with regard to what many pastors identify as one of their most important concerns—their families. It is all too easy for a pastor to spend so much time on church business that he will neglect his own family's needs; after all, he might tell himself, he's "doing it for God." Pastors' spouses may empathize with the story of the woman who said to her pastor-husband one Sunday morning, "Let's switch things around today—how about you bend over backward to make *me* happy and be grouchy with the *congregation*?"

Conclusion

These ten principles constitute a kind of structural foundation for a vibrant church community. The expectations that faithful pastors and healthy congregations have for one another all depend on these ten principles. In some sense the broad principles here describe a set of essential *shared* expectations—virtues, practices, and commitments that everyone needs to respect before discussing the specific expectations in later chapters. Hopefully, these principles are already well established in your church. Although they have aspects that may require reflection and discussion (or simple reminders), they are not likely to be particularly controversial. Who is going to take a stand against *safety* or *maturity*? To be sure, a clear *purpose* or practicing *resurrection* may be difficult for a community, but the principles themselves should not be too problematic.

In contrast, grappling with specific expectations may be a little more challenging. Some of them are not immediately obvious or uncontroversial. To help pastors and congregations discuss the expectations, chapter 2 will introduce six figures who have their own points of view. Throughout chapters 3–10, these figures will provide commentary on the expectations. Pastors and congregants are encouraged to imagine them as women and men sitting at the table in the Sunday school room and helping to get the conversation going.

Questions for You and Your Church

- Which of these ten principles seems to be most evident in your church? Which is most absent?
- Which of these would be hardest to talk about in your church? Why?
- If a stranger worshipped with your church for several weeks and attended a fellowship event or two, would he or she have a clear sense of your church's *purpose*? Why or why not?
- What does *ordination* mean to you?
- Does your church view its pastoral relationship in terms of a *covenant* or a contract?
- How is your church doing in *mutual ministry*?
- Where might your church need to let some things die so that something new might live?
- What kind of polarities or tensions characterize your church budget?
- Are there times when you or others do not feel truly safe in your church?
- *Maturity* is a life-long quest. Where do you or others in your church need to take the next step?
- In what ways are people held accountable in a loving way in your church? Where might you want to see more *accountability*?
- How is the pastor of your church maintaining *boundaries* that are healthy for everyone?

2
Six Guides for You and Your Church

This book provides reflections on the fifty-six expectation statements of chapters 3–10 through six composite characters: three laypeople (whom I call Rita, Lisa, and Ed) and three clergypersons (whom I call Dennis, Bill, and Ann). These six figures (three women and three men) represent a variety of personal and professional backgrounds. Their churches are small and large, urban and rural. They belong to a variety of denominations. Each character is particularly passionate about one or more of this book's ten principles for a vibrant church community (discussed in chapter 1). Indeed, it was in my conversations with the real people who contributed to the composite characters that the ten principles—such as *accountability, boundaries,* and *eustress*—first emerged as the central themes of this book. Together, these six characters provide diverse perspectives on how churches and pastors can thrive together.

Each of the six people is an imagined composite. Dennis and the others do not actually exist, but each of them represents the real voices of many different people, people who have spoken to me about their dreams, frustrations, experiences, and insights in the hope that churches and pastors can thrive together in a covenantal relationship. These characters emerged primarily from informal conversations and formal interviews, but I've also drawn from surveys, articles, books, and my own experiences in churches, theological education, and denominational governance. These figures represent the voices of real people, men and women who care deeply not only about their own churches but also about other churches and other pastors. Some of the quotations are taken verbatim from one of my conversations with a church leader; others are paraphrases of one particular person's thought, or reformulations of what several people were saying.

These are the real voices of people who speak passionately about God's hope for our churches. They may at times seem wise, generous, thoughtful, cranky, aggressive, or harsh, because these are ways Christians sometimes feel about their own churches. They share their reflections from the perspectives of both success and disappointment. They have learned from their mistakes, and they want others to make better choices than their own churches made.

Just as different people in a congregation give different advice, so, too, will the six voices in this book. Indeed, sometimes the statements of one person conflict with those of another. Readers will need to reflect on which pieces of advice, if any, are most appropriate for their church. The divergent or even contrary views are included because each church situation is different. You may well find yourself arguing with Ann, Dennis, or the others; such "arguments," as well as the questions at the end of each chapter, will help you clarify your own sense of what your church needs.

Although churches often share many common features and dynamics, each church has its own unique history. Churches have different liturgical styles, sizes, ages and races represented in their membership, budgets, levels of anxiety, missions, geographic locations, experiences with pastors, denominational governing structures, leadership styles, and menus for Wednesday night dinners. (Indeed, not all churches have their fellowship dinners on Wednesday night!) The perspectives shared by the six composite figures in this book will not apply equally to every congregation.

In the same way, just as no advice fits all churches, no piece of advice fits all Christians. God grants diverse gifts of the Spirit in order to equip the church as a whole for its faithful service (see 1 Corinthians 12–14). God gives to some the gift of sustained contemplative prayer, to others ability to administrate effectively, and to others a joyfulness that relieves the anxiety of those around them.

You—as both an individual and as a member of a group—are invited to see yourself or parts of yourself in these composite characters. Can Rita, a spiritual director, encourage you to bring your own deep prayer life to a committee meeting? Or do you find that too many of the leaders in your church are already like Rita, and, consequently, the church faces difficulties in effective, efficient day-to-day operations? You are also invited to learn from characters who are both similar to and quite different from you. You may or may not be involved in business, but do you have something to learn from Ed, a businessman?

Ed, a businessman

"The church needs to be run like a business—but not like any old business. It's a unique kind of business, a business that offers something nothing else can—the gospel of Jesus Christ for the forgiveness of sins."

Ed is a businessman who makes his living by being able to make hard decisions that affect people's lives. He always wears a suit to church, except on church workdays.

When his business was hurting, he kept workers on as long as felt he could, but he eventually had to make the decision to let some people go in order to keep the company afloat. That was several years ago, and he has never regretted his actions. (In most things in life, Ed does not look back.)

Ed grew up in a small town in a large family. He is the oldest son of a plumber who was, before he developed Alzheimer's disease, an active churchman. Ed likes to joke that what he learned from his dad about church was the importance of keeping the fresh water flowing and getting rid of the waste products as efficiently as possible. He believes in clear, effective processes. He is rational, practical, and efficient.

Ed believes that part of keeping things flowing smoothly is making sure the church puts the pastor in a position to succeed. As an employer, he recognizes the importance of clear job descriptions and structures for reviewing performance and professional development. Ed recognizes and respects the limits of his expertise. He wants his pastor to be better at pastoral work than he is, just as he wants his accountant to know more about accounting than he does. He would not respect the pastor if this were not the case. Although Ed contributes a substantial amount to the church each year, he does not feel like he is in any way employing the pastor. Indeed, he respects the differences between hiring an employee and calling a pastor.

Ed is fierce in his loyalty to his church because of how the pastor and some lay leaders helped save his marriage. Ed has seen the power of the gospel in his life. He knows what it means to ask for forgiveness and to be forgiven. He believes in *accountability* and *resurrection*. He trusts that God can be at work in any situation, but only when people get their emotions and egos out of the way.

Lisa, a pharmacist

"There is so much that people go through. I don't see how anyone can make it through a personal crisis without the church, without all the prayers and the friends."

Lisa is about to become a grandparent for the first time! Though she is close to retirement age and often feels tired and overworked, she very much enjoys her work as a pharmacist. She views her work as a ministry, a form of Christian service. (Not surprisingly, she loves the prayers for healing and wholeness in her church.) She is deeply concerned about how people can be disempowered simply by not knowing about things that affect them. She wants to make sure people who come to the pharmacy get all the information they need about medicines and side effects so they can have more control over their lives and have a greater sense of personal agency.

Lisa believes in seeing the best in people, particularly among people in church. She trusts that people can do the right thing, if they are patient and work together for a common good. She taught Sunday school in the past, but learned that teaching young people was not her calling. She often feels like she should be doing more in church (though no one else thinks of her this way).

Lisa's compassion and optimism is remarkable, given the recent history of her church. Several years ago, the former pastor left under circumstances that were never fully explained. There were rumors of all sorts, and some people really wanted the pastor to stay. Many people felt betrayed, either by the pastor or by their fellow church members; some, including Lisa's son and his family, left the church altogether. Loyal to her church, Lisa was part of a leadership team that had many meetings and listening sessions. She tried her best to remain calm throughout all of this mess, even though she was hurt, too. Still, she trusted that her church of many decades was where she was supposed to be—and she eventually witnessed genuine healing. (Many in the church give her some of the credit for this.) She hopes the birth of her grandchild may lead her son's family to return to the church.

Lisa is most concerned about *boundaries* and *safety*. Her optimism is grounded in attentive respect for the proper ways of doing things. If people have the right information and avoid things that are contraindicated (to use the language of Lisa's profession), good outcomes will result.

Rita, a spiritual director

"If women and men make the time to listen to God, they will hear God speaking directly to their hearts. And if they can overcome their fears, they will come to know the power of the Spirit."

Rita served as the primary caregiver as her elder sister was dying from breast cancer. She became interested in spiritual direction at the prompting of her brother, who was amazed at Rita's ability to help other family members and friends through the anguish.

Rita observed that people responded to her sister's dying in many different ways. She did a great deal of listening as visitors came to the family home; during quiet evenings, she found herself reflecting on how there could be so many different reactions to her sister's illness and death. As she later came to understand during her training as a spiritual director, she was developing the discipline of perception, learning what to look for in a person's soul, discerning the unique wear and tear of a person's life as well as the particular callings a person could be gifted for. As an avid gardener with a love of the outdoors, she always respected the distinctive conditions of light, soil, and climate that make for healthy plants. She understood that each garden has its own unique qualities. Now she was seeing that the same could be said of people.

She remains attentive to suffering and believes people often develop their awareness of God through a deep agony. She encourages people to cry out like Job, trusting that God will honor such a cry. She believes God willingly bestows courage, and she constantly encourages people to listen to Jesus when he says, "Do not be afraid." She herself has an intuitive, even mystical orientation; under different circumstances she might have become a nun.

As a spiritual director, Rita works with both laypeople and pastors. It breaks her heart to hear stories of pastors who are unable to shepherd their flocks effectively because they are emotionally needy. She sees people who engage in ministry in order to meet their own emotional needs as dangers to the church. (She put her own needs aside when caring for her sister.) She believes her call to help pastors really listen to their hearts so they can determine what they are truly called to do (including, perhaps, leaving ordained ministry).

Because she sometimes directs pastors who are not quite prepared for the responsibilities of spiritual leadership, she is most concerned with *maturity* and *boundaries*. Although her heart is heavy from hearing so many difficult life stories, she derives great joy from hearing about God at work in other people's lives. She really, really wants to hear more good stories from pastors!

Dennis, a bishop

"I want the churches under my care to be honest with me when we meet. But first, they have to be honest with themselves."

Dennis grew up on a farm in the Midwest. He believes in clear, even blunt, speech. His mother, who raised four other kids, abided by the parenting philosophy of "spare the rod, spoil the child." In her home, you learned quickly from your mistakes. He learned to respect such discipline from his mother. Loving the churches under his care, he believes his form of service sometimes requires urging churches to make very difficult decisions. Taking his office very seriously, he aspires to the high standards for bishops set forth in 1 Timothy 3 and Titus 1.

When Dennis visits a church, he often speaks on the "broken window theory of crime." Neighborhoods go into decline, sociologists say, because criminals notice that no one is fixing the broken windows in the area. Drug dealers then conclude that no one cares enough to stop them from moving in. Dennis talks about the signs that a church is going into decline, signs like long-deferred maintenance and the lack of a clear mission. He will challenge even apparently healthy churches to prove that the gospel is better served by their remaining open rather than by merging with another church.

Dennis himself is overworked, with many of his different churches experiencing challenges of all sorts. He focuses on getting people "to say what they mean and mean what they say." Dennis is protective of the pastors in his care, believing that in the absence of clear expectations and goals, a church will be more likely to evaluate its pastor on the basis of personal feelings rather than on whether she is actually leading faithfully. And he is concerned that pastors in these situations will try too hard to please the congregation (rather than helping the congregation to please God).

Dennis expects that all churches need to be attentive to conflict, brokenness, and sin, so he believes in fostering direct, honest communication. People who are honest with one another form a powerful bond of trust. And Dennis believes churches that do the hard work of establishing a clear sense of *purpose* and setting definite objectives can thrive.

A frequent reader of books on church history, Dennis is intrigued by the ways in which communities of Christians have dedicated themselves to the gospel and gone out on a limb for something special, something even radical. Sometimes a religious community can thrive for generations under the leadership of a St. Francis or a Dorothy Day. At other times, there is catastrophic failure. Although the office of bishop often seems like an office devoted to risk management, he would like to see churches take more risks for the sake of the gospel—a gospel that is, after all, pretty radical.

Dennis's commitment to getting churches on the right track leads him to be particularly attentive to the themes of *purpose* and *covenant*. Churches with a clear mission led by pastors with a clear calling are able to thrive and provide a great witness in their communities.

Ann, a young pastor

"This is my first church, and the people are so wonderful."

Ann has lots of energy and enthusiasm in her first pastorate. Throughout high school, college, and seminary, she had terrific support from her home congregation, a large church with all kinds of programs. She is eager to do well in her first church, a small, rural congregation. She senses all kinds of possibilities. Fortunately, she has not been "burned" by a bad or heart-breaking experience, and can't understand why some of her friends from seminary are having a hard time. Her husband of two years is trying to figure out what a clergy-husband should do. He sings bass and is one of the few men in the choir. They are thinking of having children, but she wants to wait until her ministry has gotten off to a good start.

She is outgoing and speaks easily in front of people. Although she is not contemplative or bookish, she has a clear set of biblical principles. The New Testament tells us how things should be in the church! Her congregation responds well to her genuineness. She is not a person of guile; she is honest and open with her thoughts, and brings out the best in others.

Ann is cautious about providing pastoral care because she believes she does not have many life experiences yet. She is not sure what to look for in people (and she did not take a pastoral care course in seminary), but trusts that reading the Bible together and praying sincerely go a long way.

Ann was nervous about her first funeral as pastor of the church. She had been there only two weeks when Emmie, a longtime leader of the congregation, died after a long illness. Ann had known Emmie was dying, so she'd taken the time to visit with her in her first few days as pastor. Nevertheless, she felt she'd stumbled through speaking with the family, preached an awkward funeral sermon, and generally could have done a much better job with everything. But a leading member of the church pointed out to her that Emmie felt comfortable enough with Ann as her pastor that she could die in peace. And her husband pointed out that many people in the church said how lovely it was that Ann was able to preach so well without knowing Emmie very long at all. Ann often thanks God for Emmie in her prayers.

Ann is excited about being a pastor and wants to get her people involved in all sorts of things. For her, *mutual ministry* and *ordination* are where it's at!

Bill, a senior pastor

"People need the gospel, not entertainment or self-help programs. People need the church to be the church."

After decades in pastoral ministry, Bill is now the very successful pastor of a large multi-staff church. Born in a small, southern town, he followed in the family footsteps; his father was a preacher, as was his granduncle. He now oversees a complex administration and has to provide guidance to young pastors (they have a two-year transition to ministry program). He has a Doctor of Ministry degree from a leading school, and is often asked to speak at events. He does not lack confidence.

Bill says the most formative part of his ministry was caring for the boiler and air handler at his first church, where he served for seven years. This was hands-on work with a finicky piece of equipment that did not always behave the way the manual said it should. Sometimes the motor just wouldn't turn. Sometimes the air just moved wherever it wanted to, despite his best efforts to manage the air registers. But the church was committed to this piece of equipment, and Bill took this as a symbol of how God is committed to us and how he should be a pastor. Pastors preach the good news, but they do so for a community of people who may or may not be working right. God does not discard what isn't working right but, with love, determination, and hope, is always tending and repairing what is broken.

Bill believes that faithful pastors can make a difference. The gospel is sufficient; God will lead people to new, abundant life if the pastor does not get in the way. He is concerned, therefore, about "wishy-washy pastors" who seem to place more value on contemporary psychology than on the power of the gospel. A good sermon has real power to heal.

Bill's strength comes in part from his willingness to learn from his own failures. He knows more than anyone else the mistakes he's made. Particularly painful for him is the memory of taking sides with the music director in a dispute with the director of Christian education. It did not seem that way at the time, but he later recognized his error—and vowed not to repeat it. Outwardly confident but inwardly humble, Bill ministers more selflessly at this point in his career. He has accomplished much of what he wanted to do as a pastor and has been able to let go of those goals that he did not achieve. His sermon titled "Be More Interested in God than You Are in Yourself" describes where he is in his own life.

Bill is particularly attentive to *eustress* and *maturity*. He knows that a healthy pastor, one who balances life's stresses and exhibits the personal wisdom that keeps the ego in check, can be a great gift to the community.

Questions for You and Your Church

- Do you see parts of yourself in one or more of these six characters? Which ones?
- Which of these composite characters do you think you will enjoy hearing from the most? Why?
- Who do you think you will learn the most from? Why?
- Do any of the women and men presented in this chapter remind you of particular people in your church? In what ways?
- Which of these characters would you most like to have in your church? Why?
- Think of an issue facing your church currently. What might these characters say about it? What advice can you imagine them giving?

Part II
**What Healthy Congregations
Expect from Faithful Pastors**

Introduction
WHAT IT'S LIKE TO BE A PASTOR

One challenge facing pastors and congregations is the simple fact that not everyone in a congregation understands what it is like to be a pastor. (Similarly, pastors often make the mistake of thinking everyone should think like they do!) Sometimes the life of a pastor is viewed as a kind of mysterious, "otherly" realm, too lofty or holy for everyone else. On the other hand, laypeople sometimes joke that being a pastor is easy since pastors work only one day a week. How can laypeople and pastors develop a *covenant* together, if neither one knows what the other really needs as together they strive to live out God's call?

The three chapters of part II describe what healthy congregations expect from faithful pastors. In order for church members to have realistic expectations of their pastor, they need to have some idea of what being a pastor is actually like. Every pastor and every church is unique, but the following glimpses might help laypeople understand what pastors like Bill, Ann, and Dennis experience as the person in the front of the sanctuary on Sunday morning.

- Pastors are the public face of the congregation, but they are not members of that congregation. They are at the center of a church, but *ordination* also sets them apart from the church.
- Pastors find that some of the most important work they do, including counseling people in crisis, concerns things they simply can't tell anyone about (or at least they shouldn't tell anyone about).
- Pastors absorb the tragedies, grief, and anguish of a congregation. When a pastor's head hits the pillow at night, it is filled with thoughts and prayers for all the needs of the congregation. This can make sleep difficult. Pastors may feel the need to intercede on behalf of the people as Moses did, or simply to cry out like Job.
- Pastors often experience isolation, especially if the congregation lacks a strong sense of *mutual ministry*. The pastor is often the only full-time staff in a community of part-time volunteers, and she may or may not have meaningful collegial relationships with other local clergy.

- Pastoral service is born of hope and love. Pastors want the best for their congregations. Pastors will make mistakes and often have mixed motives, but the vast majority really do want the best for the people in their care.
- Pastors are more likely to be willing to take risks than the congregation. Most pastors do not plan on staying at a church for the rest of their lives or being buried there, so they are willing to take risks to see what the church could become. Believing the church and its members would be better off if everyone volunteered a little more and gave a little more money, pastors sometimes want more for their congregants than the congregants seem to want for themselves.
- A layperson said, "I just don't know how our pastor preaches a sermon each and every week"—and many pastors don't quite know either![1] Struggling to prepare meaningful sermons week in and week out, some pastors wonder, "Is anyone listening?" They need feedback (especially constructive criticism) and encouragement if they are to sustain what Episcopal priest and author Barbara Brown Taylor calls "the preaching life."[2]
- A pastor is responsible for the well-being of everyone in the congregation. This includes members of the congregation she personally may not like and members who make life difficult for her.
- In terms of both time and money, pastors often feel torn between the well-being of their families and the well-being of the congregation. A congregation often expects its pastor to be a "spiritual" person, but he also has very real material needs, such as a home, healthy food, clothes, and possibly educational expenses for children.
- Pastors' schedules can be maddeningly unpredictable. Who knows when the phone will ring with an emergency that demands that the pastor leave his daughter's softball game?
- Pastors are responsible for many different things, including visiting the sick and dying, preaching and leading worship, preparing people for marriage (or divorce), offering prayers at social events, teaching the young and the old, reaching out to new members, encouraging volunteers, connecting with the community, strategic planning, overseeing budgets, and administering an institution. In addition, pastors sometimes take on tasks that others in the church could be doing (such as repairing the plumbing). No pastor is good at everything, and many pastors are downright uncomfortable in some of these situations. Pastors, particularly solo pastors, need the discipline of *boundaries* and *accountability*. It is all too easy for pastors to do what they enjoy doing or feel comfortable doing while neglecting the things they really need to do, the things the congregation may expect them to do.
- The "fit" between pastor and congregation is mysterious. Sometimes good, faithful pastors with wonderful gifts for ministry end up in good, faithful

churches with wonderful gifts for ministry—and things still don't work out. Personality, worship styles, theology, politics—any of these could get in the way of what might otherwise be a long pastorate.

- A pastor needs to be clear about his own theology while, at the same time, meeting people where they are in their own understandings of who God is. Pastors are sometimes expected to have the answers, but they run the risk of imposing their own views on congregants.

- Like everyone else, pastors like to be liked. But sometimes (also like everyone else), they are responsible for doing what is right rather than what is popular.

- At its best, the pastoral life is a life that really matters. Pastors are privileged to be involved with people's lives at important times, and grateful to have the opportunity to make a difference.

As these glimpses suggest, pastors are human—just like laypeople. Serving as a pastor can be a great joy as well as a significant challenge. All pastors need help from their congregations. Stress is inevitable, but in a healthy congregation it can become *eustress*. Covenantal help with both *accountability* and setting *boundaries* is also essential. One of the greatest gifts congregation and pastors can give each other is mutually agreed-upon expectations. When expectations are clear, it is far easier for pastors to keep the inevitable *eustress* tensions in tune and to sustain a life of service.

3
Theology and Worship
FOCUSING ON GOD

Despite its title, this chapter is not a discussion of what congregations should expect of their pastors in terms of specific theological beliefs or approaches to worship. Rather, this chapter is about the importance of keeping a focus on God first and foremost in the life of the church, about making sure Christians do not look at the church from a purely "human point of view" (2 Corinthians 5:16).

Too often, churches substitute institutional habits for a vital relationship with the living God. It is easy for a pastor to become an organizer and manager whose primary concern is to keep his members happy. Similarly, it is easy for congregations to set low standards for themselves and their leaders, and for such communities to let squabbles and pessimism dominate. But when churches and pastors genuinely keep God first, they are able to move away from their own ego needs or anxieties and focus on what is truly important—their God-given *purpose.*

To be sure, encountering the living God can be frightening for Christians today, just as it was for Moses and Paul. God promises so much more than basic contentment. And God expects so much more than checking in for an hour every other Sunday. But churches that have the courage to hunger for God's Word and the hopefulness to speak with God from their hearts can thrive. Healthy congregations expect their faithful pastors to help them do just these things.

Healthy congregations expect faithful pastors . . .
3.1 – to understand that ministry is about serving God, not about themselves.
3.2 – to have "pastoral imagination" and to view the church and the congregation theologically.
3.3 – to desire more for their congregations without becoming brokenhearted.
3.4 – to encourage others to have high hopes and to push the church to do its very best.
3.5 – to discern models of ministry relevant to their particular churches.
3.6 – to preach on difficult subjects, even if it makes them unpopular.
3.7 – to lead the people in worshipping the living God.

3.1 Healthy congregations expect faithful pastors . . .
to understand that ministry is about serving God, not about themselves.

"Our ministries themselves are not redemptive. Only the ministry of Jesus is redemptive."[1]

—Andrew Purves

THE BEST PASTORS PRACTICE what they preach. Pastors preach the love of God, affirming from the pulpit that nothing "will be able to separate us from the love of God in Christ Jesus our Lord" (Romans 8:39). Pastors teach the importance of giving the glory to God and living lives of thankful response. The best pastors live this out on a daily basis, focusing on what God is up to rather than what they are doing.

But when a person is doing God's work, there is a temptation that is hard to resist. Ministry is a form of power, and all forms of power bring temptations and the potential for abuse. Where does serving God stop and ego gratification begin? In *The Crucifixion of Ministry*, scholar Andrew Purves articulates two central themes that speak directly to pastors who tend to focus on the importance of their own efforts: "1. Conceiving ministry as *our* ministry is the root problem of what ails us in ministry today. 2. Ministry should be understood as a sharing in the continuing ministry of Jesus Christ, for wherever Christ is, there is the church and her ministry."[2]

When the pastor assumes unconsciously that ministry is about her and what she is doing (even when such actions are done in God's name), she easily begins to be anxious about church attendance or other measures of "success." At its worst, pastors can come to feel that their self-worth comes almost entirely from the success of "their" ministries. (The next chapter addresses this problem directly.) Motivated by her own ego, the pastor worries that "her" church will simply be like so many others that failed to thrive and ultimately entered into decline. Anxiety, sorrow, and lamentation can become powerful residents in her soul. And when church life is not thriving, some pastors may look for someone to blame, perhaps themselves or the congregation. Publicly in meetings or privately in her own soul, the pastor begins to judge the congregation (or particular members), condemning them for not agreeing with her idea for a ministry that would revolutionize the church.

Ann the young pastor says,
"One of the great gifts a congregation can give me is to affirm the work of God in the church. I am most pleased—and better supported—if the congregation says 'We see God here' instead of 'You are doing such wonderful things.'"

Bill the senior pastor says,
"Congregations need to remember that they are calling a John the Baptist, not a Jesus. In many of the old paintings, John is pointing away from himself, often in the direction of something you can't see in the painting. That's my role as a pastor—to point others to Jesus. Pastors need to remember John's words, 'He must increase, but I must decrease' (John 3:30)."

Rita the spiritual director says,
"I am always concerned when I hear a pastor speak to me of 'my ministry.' That phrase makes me stop and wonder if the pastor has the right motivations. Often, it is just a phrase used without much thought, but sometimes it reveals a deeply needy person—and that can be a danger for Christian ministry."

Healthy congregations thrive because their pastors consistently keep everyone's attention on Christ. Faithful pastors thrive because their congregations are focused on God.

Pastors, like most other professionals, wish to see their financial and social rewards go up over the course of their vocational lives. For this reason, pastors may be tempted to equate keeping the congregation happy (which helps their careers) with doing God's work. Faithful pastors who consistently put God first in theology and practice are able to avoid not only the temptations of the ego but also the temptations of building a "career."

At my church, this Expectation is:

__**Not** Discussed	__**Not** Practiced
__**Not Widely** Agreed Upon	__**Not Widely** Practiced
__**Somewhat** Agreed Upon	__**Somewhat** Practiced
__**Widely** Agreed Upon	__**Widely** Practiced
__**Not** Applicable	__**Not** Applicable

3.2 Healthy congregations expect faithful pastors . . .
to have "pastoral imagination" and to view the church and the congregation thelogically.

"Life lived long enough and fully enough in the pastoral office gives rise to a way of seeing in depth and of creating new realities that is an indispensible to the church . . . and indeed to public life and to the world."[3]

—Craig Dykstra

MOST PASTORS LIKE TO "fit in" with the congregation. Like everyone else, they enjoy comfortable social relationships built around shared pleasures and a common way of looking at things. But *ordination* sets a person apart, and one aspect of being set apart is to view people, the church, and its mission from a distinctively theological perspective.

Churches have pastors because they need to be led by people who spend extended time with God in prayer and Scripture. They need leaders who know the extensive history of the church and the wisdom gained by men and women over the centuries as they have sought to follow God. Churches need pastors who consider everything from the perspective of the gospel, not the perspectives of TV, popular culture, political slogans, or the latest business model. After all, the Bible speaks frequently of "the ways of the Lord" (Psalm 18:21), contrasting these with the ways of the world.

Pastors are called by both God and the church to view their communities in terms of the fundamentals of Christian theology: sin and grace, death and *resurrection*, the goodness and holiness of the Creator. Pastors are called to see everyone—including themselves and the most devout people in the pews—as sinners in need of God's mercy. Pastors are called to see the present in light of God's eternal kingdom. Thus, pastors are called to see that there is a theological problem, for example, with all-white congregations in racially or ethnically diverse neighborhoods.

Pastors look not only to what God has done in the past but also to the future that God is creating in the church's midst. Scholar Craig Dykstra speaks of "pastoral imagination" as that quality that discerns what God is intending and, in turn, seeks to create ways for the congregation to participate in that. Pastors thus share an affinity with

Ed the businessman says,
"I want a pastor with the courage to challenge me. It's a waste of good money for her to do otherwise. I can get therapy and entertainment elsewhere. I want the gospel—and this means I need someone who cares more about God than about keeping me happy."

Lisa the pharmacist says,
"What makes our church so wonderful is the fact that so many of us are doing what it says in the Pentecost story in Acts 2—having visions about what God is doing in our community, dreaming about where we could be heading. It's not just the pastor who is on fire for what could be."

Ann the young pastor says,
"When I was in seminary, I discovered that novels, movies, and music really shaped my ability to read the Bible. When a professor asked me to imagine casting different actresses to play the role of Mary Magdalene, she wasn't talking about movies but inviting me more deeply into the Bible. Cultivating my imagination through the arts is one of the best ways for me to understand my congregation and its call."

painters, writers, and musicians, for these men and women, too, are led to see differently. And pastors are called to help congregants see differently, to help them develop what Dykstra calls the "ecclesial imagination" of the church.[4]

On the lookout for the in-breaking of the kingdom of God, faithful pastors seek to discern where God is leading the congregation, to see what God is calling into being before it is there, perhaps even before it is dreamed of.

Congregations risk change whenever they call a pastor. A faithful pastor honors what God has done in a community, even as he evaluates the present mission of the church in light of God's future. And such a way of seeing may well lead to changes in a church.

At my church, this Expectation is:

__**Not** Discussed	__**Not** Practiced
__**Not Widely** Agreed Upon	__**Not Widely** Practiced
__**Somewhat** Agreed Upon	__**Somewhat** Practiced
__**Widely** Agreed Upon	__**Widely** Practiced
__**Not** Applicable	__**Not** Applicable

3.3 Healthy congregations expect faithful pastors . . .
to desire more for their congregations without becoming brokenhearted.

"Expect great things from God. Attempt great things for God."

-—William Carey (1761-1834), missionary to India

FAITHFUL PASTORS HAVE high hopes for the congregations they serve. They recognize that God is at work in the midst of the people. They dream of what churches could do if pastors preach faithfully and the laity responds with enthusiasm and concerted action. Most pastors I interviewed believe that if every church member were a little bit more active, and if everyone gave a little bit more money, their churches could do even greater things for God. Healthy churches respect this and joyfully serve God with a pastor who calls, prods, and encourages them to do the best they possibly can in responding to God's call. (For more on this, see the next section.)

Unfortunately, not all pastors and churches end up in such a happy condition. Sometimes pastors passionately want the best for "their" people, but the people do not respond with the same intensity, or do not agree with the pastor about the wisdom of his initiatives. Pastors in such circumstances may simply grow weary in well doing and lose their energy for ministry (see Galatians 6:9). They may have lost their sense of *purpose*, or they may simply be exhausted from trying to do too much (see the dangers of "over-functioning" in 5.2). In such situations, striving for excellence seems almost impossible.

For pastors, having expectations for their churches that are too high can thus lead to clergy burnout or clergy heartbreak. Clergy whose hearts have been broken by an experience with a congregation sometimes subtly shift their hopes downward. No one likes having his heart broken twice, so a pastor may unconsciously seek to protect himself by assuming that a congregation should not try to do too much. Such pastors stop hungering for more and accept the status quo—things are good enough. Fearful of leading, these pastors find *safety* in managing.

Lisa the pharmacist says,
"There are some people who pick up their prescriptions with a really sad look on their face, as if nothing will ever make a difference. I was serving Communion once, and I saw the same look on some people's faces. How do pastors deal with such a lack of enthusiasm?"

Dennis the bishop says,
"The greatest threats to pastoral energy and enthusiasm come from unrealistic expectations. The pastor expects too much of the church, or the congregation puts all their expectations on the pastor— the new pastor is going to increase membership, get the youth involved in church, solve the budget problem, and so on. How can a pastor meet all these expectations, especially if the congregation's expectations are his responsibility? Great expectations are wonderful—but they need to be realistic. The challenge is: How do you know when something is 'realistic'? God is always surprising us with increasing our sense of what's possible."

Bill the senior pastor says,
"I see two things too much—young pastors who are too eager and seasoned pastors who have already given up. The former have no idea of the power of sin, and the latter have no idea of the power of God."

Effective ministry requires risk taking. (Much of the discussion about servant-leadership in chapter 5 focuses on taking risks.) And the gospel calls Christians to boldness, confidence, and hope. Sometimes faith makes it possible to achieve something no one thought possible. At other times, blindly pursuing a dream can be destructive of the pastor and the congregation. The essential question always remains: What is God doing?

At my church, this Expectation is:

__**Not** Discussed   __**Not** Practiced
__**Not Widely** Agreed Upon   __**Not Widely** Practiced
__**Somewhat** Agreed Upon   __**Somewhat** Practiced
__**Widely** Agreed Upon   __**Widely** Practiced
__**Not** Applicable   __**Not** Applicable

3.4 Healthy congregations expect faithful pastors . . .
to encourage others to have high hopes and to push the church to do its very best.

"To lead is to help a community articulate an exciting possible future and to pursue that future as the purpose of its existence."[5]

—George B. Thompson Jr.

FAITHFUL PASTORS HAVE great hopes for their congregations. Healthy congregations, too, look forward to "an exciting possible future." But not all churches sustain such enthusiasm and hope.

For a variety of reasons, churches can be particularly vulnerable to being complaisant, to accepting a low level of personal effort, sacrifice, or risk. Paul says we have been "justified by faith" (Romans 3:28). But if we are already justified (made right with God), what else is there to do besides show up Sunday morning and give thanks? Further, are we not also warned by Jesus about self-righteousness and by Paul of the dangers of works-righteousness? With such important biblical statements shaping our lives as Christians, it is sometimes all too easy to focus on God's work and ignore Jesus' call to "be perfect as your heavenly father is perfect" (Matthew 5:48). Or sometimes such perfection seems like too high a standard. We are concerned that if we set high standards for church life, people may go to the church next door that asks less of its members. For their part, pastors may be cautious about asking congregants to give more of their time or money. Won't the congregation resent that?

Many Christians may genuinely wonder why they are not making any progress as disciples or providing the kind of meaningful witness they want to offer in their community. Athletes train hard to discover just how good they can be. Knowing full well that progress does not always come easily, they push themselves so they can discover what their best really is. Paul uses sports metaphors for Christians—and the saying is true for both bodybuilders and body-of-Christ builders: no pain, no gain. Good athletes are grateful when the coach requires them to do even more wind sprints, because such coaches are often able to get them to do something they never thought they could do. As

Rita the spiritual director says,
"People don't like to share their deepest hopes. They are very personal, and we risk disappointment if the other person does not share or respect them. But Christians have common hopes, and beautiful and holy things happen when Christians speak from the heart and share their dreams for their community. Church members don't always realize that they can strengthen their pastor and themselves by simply speaking from the heart about their hopes and dreams."

Dennis the bishop says,
"There is a saying that 'Good is the enemy of better,' and that saying holds true for churches. Many churches do things well, but sometimes they can do these same things even better. And over time, being satisfied with doing things well can lead to doing things just okay, and that can lead to stagnation and not doing things well at all. It is important to celebrate what is going well, but we need to balance that with also seeking to do things better. I encourage pastors and churches to find that balance."

one layperson said, "The more you carry a heavy object, the stronger your body gets. The more you carry a cross, the stronger your soul gets."[6]

Church is like anything else in life—the more you put in, the more you get out. Healthy congregations therefore expect their pastors to push them to discover their very best. Such communities recognize the need for leadership that challenges, energizes, encourages, and, when necessary, chides them.

Faithful pastors encourage their members to take the risks, make the sacrifices, and put in the effort needed to make genuine progress in the spiritual life, both individually and collectively.

Ed the businessman says,

"It may not be good theology, but I'd like to see pastors try to drive their churches into the kingdom of God or drive them into the ground. Come to think of it, maybe that is good theology. Didn't Jesus commission the apostles to go out and preach and tell them, 'If any place will not welcome you and they refuse to hear you, as you leave, shake the off the dust that is on your feet as a testimony against them' (Mark 6:11)? In worship I'd rather struggle with a courageous leader who expects me to get more involved than listen to a cautious manager."

At my church, this Expectation is:

__**Not** Discussed

__**Not Widely** Agreed Upon

__**Somewhat** Agreed Upon

__**Widely** Agreed Upon

__**Not** Applicable

__**Not** Practiced

__**Not Widely** Practiced

__**Somewhat** Practiced

__**Widely** Practiced

__**Not** Applicable

3.5 Healthy congregations expect faithful pastors . . .
to discern models of ministry relevant to their particular churches.

"Sometimes it seems like there are too many different kinds of things I need to do each day. I'm good at speaking with folks, but I'm really not comfortable with the business end."[7]

—a United Methodist pastor

THERE ARE MANY DIFFERENT terms we could use to speak of what pastors do. From the Bible we could use *prophet, priest, sage,* and *shepherd*. In today's language, the pastor can also be a *communicator, administrator, organizer, cheerleader, coach, manager, leader, performer, confidant, plumber, social worker,* and *advocate*.

Pastors will be gifted in some of these roles but not others. And because they are human, pastors are likely to focus on doing what they do well. (This is one aspect of the importance of *safety*—people do what they feel safe doing.) A pastor who thrives leading the people in worship—a priestly role—will dedicate more time and energy to preparing for Sunday morning. After all, the church is grounded in praise of the living God. A pastor who enjoys meeting with congregants and providing advice for life's challenges—a sage's role—will have many one-on-one meetings. After all, the church is grounded in meaningful relationships.

But faithful pastors recognize the responsibility of discernment. Each pastor is called to discern the particular needs and resources of the congregation, allowing that insight to shape the way she serves as a pastor. A disorganized church may require a pastor to spend more time in administration than she would like. Paul's example seems appropriate: he said he was willing to become as a Jew or Gentile according to the needs of the situation (1 Cor. 9:19–22).

Further, faithful pastors recognize that most of these roles will be called for over the course of their pastorates. The challenge is, first, to balance multiple pastoral roles (churches will need most of them at different times), and, second, to prioritize the roles (pastors must discern *when* to be *what*). Given a pastor's own tendencies and desires, and given that dominant personalities in a congregation may insist on having a certain type of pastor—one the rest of

Ed the businessman says,
"It drives me nuts that there are so many different expectations for the pastor in my congregation. My pastor is really good at preaching, but he is a so-so administrator. I'm grateful for the former, but I don't give him grief about the latter. Shouldn't that be part of the congregation's role—to use a thoughtful Mutual Ministry Review to figure out how we can use our abilities to address his weaknesses? A good business plan puts people in a position to thrive."

Dennis the bishop says,
"I have often wondered if we should have an office of prophet in our churches. Some pastors are called to be prophetic in ministry—and they are great at challenging, even confronting a congregation. But when we ask that person to also fulfill a priestly role and provide pastoral care, we may run into trouble. For some people, a pastor who preaches on race relations or another hot-button social issue is a meddler. And many congregants simply don't warm to meddlers. There is a side of me that would like to free my prophetic pastors up somehow. But for now, what I need to do is help find ways to help these pastors discern how effective pastoral care can be a foundation for prophetic ministry."

the congregation may not need—this ongoing work of faithful discernment can be very difficult.

Faithful pastors are prepared to serve in different roles according to the genuine needs of their congregation. And faithful pastors recognize that their time of service at a particular congregation may be drawing to a close when their gifts and graces are no longer relevant to God's call for the congregation.

Rita the spiritual director says,
"Helpful individual congregants balance their own sense of what they need from their pastor with an awareness of what the congregation as a whole needs. They speak honestly and respectfully about both, not only to the pastor but also to other members of the congregation."

At my church, this Expectation is:

__**Not** Discussed

__**Not Widely** Agreed Upon

__**Somewhat** Agreed Upon

__**Widely** Agreed Upon

__**Not** Applicable

__**Not** Practiced

__**Not Widely** Practiced

__**Somewhat** Practiced

__**Widely** Practiced

__**Not** Applicable

3.6 Healthy congregations expect faithful pastors . . .
to preach on difficult subjects, even if it makes them unpopular.

"Pastors aren't called to preach happiness. We are called to preach holiness."[8]

—a Presbyterian pastor

PASTORS KNOW THEIR CONGREGATIONS will be pleased when they preach a comforting message. But they also know God's Word includes things that God's people don't always want to hear about—topics like tithing, race relations, praying for enemies, and the sinful uses of violence for apparently good ends. While these topics are in the Bible, they may not always help the pastor win a popularity contest. When I was a student in divinity school, one professor advised us to "Duck and take cover behind the pulpit and tell your congregation, 'Don't get mad at me. Get mad at God for writing these things in the first place.'" Pastors can empathize with Paul's words in Galatians 1:10 when the apostle asks rhetorically if he is trying to win God's approval or other people's.

The purpose of preaching is sometimes summarized as "to comfort the afflicted and to afflict the comfortable." A church that is so comfortable that it resents "being afflicted" may only be getting part of the gospel. Liking Jesus as Savior but not as Lord, they might not be getting the good news at all.

But as is suggested throughout this book, the laity is more likely to be healthy, eager, and generous if the pastor focuses on what God wants to say more than what people want to hear. Part of the pastor's work is to call people to lives pleasing to God, and living in this way may require difficult personal and/or institutional changes. Such changes are easier to make when we are doing them together, particularly if we are doing them together in a church. As Christians, we expect following Christ means making these changes—and we should expect we will need help.

Healthy congregations *expect* their pastors to preach on difficult topics; indeed, maybe they even *demand* it as part of their right to hear the fullness of the gospel. Some church members may be upset, and

Bill the senior pastor says,
"I try to work with our lay leaders to help them understand that I'm going to preach on an uncomfortable subject about once a quarter. I want them to have my back, even if they disagree with me. Talking one-on-one beforehand really helps. They appreciate it when I listen to their concerns about money or racial issues before I speak. And I find that even if I'm upset about an issue, I can communicate more effectively."

Dennis the bishop says,
"Baptist pastors have confessed, when their congregants are not around, that they will not preach on some topics on Sunday morning because they do not want the Board of Deacons to fire them Sunday night. Other denominations make it impossible to 'fire' the pastor outright after a challenging sermon, but many pastors nevertheless have a hard time preaching on tough subjects. After all, a pastor depends on the goodwill of the laity if he wants healthy committees, eager volunteers, and generous givers. It's the pastor's covenantal responsibility to preach the Word faithfully, and it's the congregation's responsibility to respond covenantally—to respect the pastor's authority even when they disagree."

some may be annoyed—but in the long run the pastor and the congregation will thrive together.

Hearing faithful sermons on difficult topics strengthens a congregation because it draws a congregation deeper into the life of God and God's kingdom. Christian discipleship is not easy, but many Christians appreciate the challenge of living faithfully as a witness to God's hope.

Ann the young pastor says,
"One of the greatest things a senior lay leader in my first church did for me (and for the whole church!) was to give me a 'blank check' for my preaching. She said, 'You are here for a reason, and that is to preach the Word we can't get anywhere else. We can get self-help elsewhere, and we have service organizations aplenty. Don't hold back, dearie.'"

At my church, this Expectation is:

__**Not** Discussed
__**Not Widely** Agreed Upon
__**Somewhat** Agreed Upon
__**Widely** Agreed Upon
__**Not** Applicable

__**Not** Practiced
__**Not Widely** Practiced
__**Somewhat** Practiced
__**Widely** Practiced
__**Not** Applicable

3.7 Healthy congregations expect faithful pastors . . .
to lead the people in worshipping the living God.

"Worship is about what God wants, not what we want. That keeps everything we do in perspective."[9]

—an Episcopal layperson

WORSHIP DOES GREAT THINGS for us—that's one reason God commands it! In worship, we encounter the living God. We receive and respond. We are humbled, comforted, challenged, and startled. We have opportunities to give, to let go, to bless, and to be blessed. Worship gives us fellowship and *safety*—a place to share the full range of emotions from joy to sorrow, a community to help us grow in *maturity*. Worship orients our lives and offers a source of belonging, *purpose*, and *ministry*. We enjoy a time for reflection and discover that in God's grace we can let go of our worries. We practice *resurrection*. We are able to hear the good news that God forgives us and loves us—even as we are also held *accountable*. We relish beautiful music and find peace; a finely tuned voice helps us keep our *eustress* in tune.

There is so much potential in worship, and pastors who have primary responsibility for leading worship may confront many questions. Is the service flowing smoothly? Is it going to run too long? Will having a liturgical dance have a negative impact on the budget? Will the congregation know the next hymn (or will someone be upset by it)? Was that a scowl I just saw? Why is that person yawning? Will the visitors feel welcomed and want to come back?

Perhaps the pastor is looking out into the congregation and seeing all the difficulties and challenges people are facing—the divorces, the lost jobs, the anger, the betrayal. Maybe the pastor is concentrating on the sermon about to be delivered, wondering if his words will be God's Word. And how about his family? The pastor is not able to sit in the pews with his wife or children—so they are separated during worship's moments of great emotional intensity.

Healthy congregations recognize both the importance and the challenges of leading faithful worship, and they help the pastor help them stay focused on God.

Rita the spiritual director says,
"I remember the expressions on a group of pastors when they received Communion at a denominational gathering on clergy health. They were the assembled congregation. The sermon was preached as God's Word to them. They came to the table hungry, eager, with profound longing. The previous Sunday and for many, many Sundays before that, I imagine, each of them had been distributing the elements with confidence, their faces radiating reassurance. They were the public face of God. But now, freed from that responsibility, they were liberated to do just as Psalm 34:8 tells us: to 'taste and see that the Lord is good.' How often had the goodness of God become hidden behind their own public role as worship leaders? I'd like to see more churches have the pastor sit with them in the pews more often, allow him or her to worship with them more."

Lisa the pharmacist says,
"So much trust is involved in worship. We trust that something important is happening, even if we don't 'feel' anything. We trust that a difficult sermon—or a boring one!—actually is the Word of God. We trust that the person who messed up a committee assignment is still able to lead the prayers. We trust that something urgent is afoot—even when it seems like the same old worship service. Maybe that's the point—when we come to church on Sunday morning, we are freed from thinking it's all about us."

Charles Wesley's hymn "Love Divine, All Loves Excelling" closes with a glorious image of worship: "lost in wonder, love, and praise." Christians can indeed lose themselves in worship as they experience the majesty of God and become aware of their place and *purpose* in the world.

At my church, this Expectation is:

__**Not** Discussed   __**Not** Practiced
__**Not Widely** Agreed Upon   __**Not Widely** Practiced
__**Somewhat** Agreed Upon   __**Somewhat** Practiced
__**Widely** Agreed Upon   __**Widely** Practiced
__**Not** Applicable   __**Not** Applicable

Questions for You and Your Church

- How does your church sustain its focus on God and what God is calling the church to do?
- What signs are there, if any, that your pastor has high hopes for your congregation?
- In what ways does your congregation have high hopes for itself (or not)?
- Every church has a range of commitments—caring for the congregation, providing Christian education, maintaining the physical plant, reaching out to prospective new members, supporting the music program, nurturing the youth, and so forth. All these are valuable. If you came up with six important commitments for your church, how would people in your church or discussion group place these in order of priority?
- How has the church talked with the pastor about ways of doing ministry appropriate for the congregation?
- Does the pastor of your church preach on difficult subjects, or do you wonder if he is shying away from those? Would you like to hear more sermons that challenge you to think about giving more to the church or thinking about social issues differently? If so, how might you start a conversation in the church to encourage more of these sermons?

4

Self-Knowledge and Self-Care
PASTORS PRACTICING WHAT THEY PREACH

Pastors ask their congregants to read books, to deepen their prayer lives, to take care of their bodies, and to honor their families. Faithful pastors lead by example. To paraphrase the saying of St. Francis, pastors are preaching the gospel constantly and, when necessary, they use words. Unfortunately, some pastors are so busy that they neglect the core practices of self-knowledge and self-care required to sustain them both as people and as pastors. They don't always practice what they preach.

But healthy congregations expect their pastors to exhibit *maturity*. Indeed, one of the things that sets a faithful pastor apart is her wisdom—which includes her ability to use what she knows effectively, her acceptance of her strengths and limitations, her understanding of who she is called to be, and her remaining steady in challenging situations.[1]

The wise, mature pastor is able to look beyond his own needs and see the bigger picture. He knows that devoting time to reflection and physical exercise serves God and the congregation. As Quaker author and educator Parker J. Palmer notes, "self-care is never a selfish act."[2] Healthy congregations are glad when Paul's words apply to their own pastor, "teaching everyone in all wisdom, so that we may present everyone mature in Christ" (Colossians 1:28). Churches benefit when pastors practice what they preach.

Healthy congregations expect faithful pastors . . .
4.1 – not to take everything personally.
4.2 – to remain calm and to help promote *safety* in the church.
4.3 – to pursue holiness.
4.4 – to be learning and growing constantly.
4.5 – to be involved in a peer group for support, collaboration, and *accountability*.
4.6 – to respect their bodies as temples of the Holy Spirit.
4.7 – to be able to receive care.
4.8 – to honor their own families just as pastors encourage church members to honor theirs.
4.9 – to observe Sabbath rest.

4.1 Healthy congregations expect faithful pastors . . .
not to take everything personally.

"Without a high degree of self-awareness, we run the risk of using ministry to meet our emotional needs. The more hard-earned self-knowledge we possess the less likely we are to project onto others our insecurities and past wounds."[3]

—Mahan Siler

PEOPLE WHO STUDY CHURCHES sometimes use the words *fusion* and *differentiation* to describe "emotional process in relationships."[4] The terms refer to the ability to separate feeling and thinking in one's own mind, and the capacity to distinguish between one's own identity and responsibilities from the way others feel.

Fusion and differentiation come from family systems theory, the study of families and their behaviors.[5] Fusion describes a condition in which the people are simply too close, too enmeshed. Individuals depend on each other too much for their own well-being. A father's well-being can be so tied to his son's happiness that he becomes unable to provide proper discipline; upsetting his son is too upsetting for him.

By contrast, "the emotional maturity of differentiation allows us to think things through for ourselves."[6] People who are well differentiated can be emotionally connected but are also able to remain objective about their responsibilities. They don't take everything so personally because they realize that someone else's bad mood may have nothing to do with them—and they know "fixing" that person's mood is not their responsibility.

While differentiation can be described as one aspect of *maturity* and is needed for providing good leadership, fusion is a great temptation for pastors. Pastors get so caught up in their work that their emotional well-being can depend almost entirely on their congregations. When the people say "good job!" they feel good, but when the people do not respond with praise and gratitude, they wonder, "Am I bad pastor—or even a bad person? Why don't they like me more?"

This over-dependence on work in determining one's identity is not unique to pastors. (It may be equally true of many other people in a congregation.) But it is particularly problematic in churches because it can lead to several dangers, including over-functioning (see Expectation 5.2); codependency (see

Ann the young pastor says,
"We all want to be liked—and needed. It makes us feel good. But it took me a while to realize how that personal desire hurt the people I loved so much. I realized that I was avoiding conversations and topics that would lead to conflict, which might cause people not to like me as much. But those were conversations that needed to happen. The problems did not go away."

Bill the senior pastor says,
"I have to admit that in my first pastorate, I loved the congregation selfishly. I loved them because I wanted them to love me back. But I was so hurt when we had a disagreement over a new ministry. I took it personally, because I felt like it was about me rather than about the church or God or serving others. Over the years, I have tried to love my other congregations as selflessly as possible. The New Testament speaks of a special kind of love, agape, a self-sacrificial love. That's very different from the love that needs something in return."

10.5); and increased congregational anxiety (see the next section of this chapter).

Grounding themselves in God, faithful pastors practice prayerful self-reflection and self-care. They seek clarity about their own emotional needs and responsibilities. They remain deeply engaged with their congregations, caring without getting caught up (fused) with members' happiness. Not taking every-thing personally, they respect constructive criticism and can guide the congregation through conflict.

Although churches like to feel close—indeed, close like a family—church leaders, and especially the pastor, need the *maturity* that comes from differentiation. Not taking everything person-ally is a gift to everyone.

Lisa the pharmacist says,
"Back when we were dealing with various problems, a number of us read Ronald Richardson's Creating a Healthier Church *so we could learn more about emotional systems, anxiety, triangles, patterns of reactivity—those kinds of things. A lot of light bulbs went on! We could see ourselves and our problems much more clearly. It was kind of painful, to be honest, but it helped."*

At my church, this Expectation is:

__**Not** Discussed   __**Not** Practiced
__**Not Widely** Agreed Upon   __**Not Widely** Practiced
__**Somewhat** Agreed Upon   __**Somewhat** Practiced
__**Widely** Agreed Upon   __**Widely** Practiced
__**Not** Applicable   __**Not** Applicable

4.2 Healthy congregations expect faithful pastors . . .
to remain calm and to help promote safety in the church.

"All shall be well, and all shall be well, and all manner of things shall be well."
—Julian of Norwich, early fifteenth-century Christian mystic

WHEN PEOPLE COME TO church, they may bring with them any number of challenges, including crises in health, finances, or relationships. Churches are emotionally intense places, charged with the power of the Spirit and shaped by politics, finances, displaced hopes and fears, and many underlying, often unstated needs. Chronic or acute anxiety is not uncommon, and church life is often governed by unconscious emotional needs. It should not be surprising that some churches exhibit "fight or flight" or "passive-aggressive" behavior (see Expectation 10.1).

It is to this group of people that Jesus says, "Do not be afraid." One aspect of the gospel is that even though life presents many challenges, we do not have to live in fear. We can rest secure in the providential love of God.

For this good news to be heard and believed by their congregations, church leaders need to walk the walk in their daily lives. If the pastor is anxious, the congregation will pick up on that and, probably, will reflect it back to the pastor. If the pastor is a calm, non-anxious presence, the congregation will feel more secure. Such a pastor will help others see God's love in the midst of distressing times.

Chapter 1 stated that *safety* is required for a vibrant church community, and that it should not be taken for granted. Churches should be places where people can feel truly safe and live in hope, not fear.

Church leaders cannot control the emotions of the members of their congregations, but they can have a decisive influence. Hence, a pastor who exhibits emotional *maturity* can be a great gift to the congregation.

Rita the spiritual director says,
"Each person who remains calm and steady, everyone who brings to church meetings or parking lot conversations an abiding trust in the goodness of God, everyone who shares the vision of Julian of Norwich that, indeed, with God's help 'all shall be well'—each of these people contributes to the overall health of the congregation. The pastor and lay leaders in particular need to align their sight with Julian's. She was not naïve or simply optimistic—no, she saw all too clearly the sorrows of Jesus. But she also saw the power of God's love to make all things right."

Lisa the pharmacist says,
"One of the things our congregation learned from Ronald Richardson's Creating a Healthier Church *was that you can be a calming presence in an anxious situation by simply being curious. If you ask questions and take a genuine interest in what people think and how they feel—and do so without judging others or letting your own feelings get in the way—people relax a bit. Remaining objective and asking clear questions encourages others to become less reactive and more reflective."*

At my church, this Expectation is:

__**Not** Discussed
__**Not Widely** Agreed Upon
__**Somewhat** Agreed Upon
__**Widely** Agreed Upon
__**Not** Applicable

__**Not** Practiced
__**Not Widely** Practiced
__**Somewhat** Practiced
__**Widely** Practiced
__**Not** Applicable

Ed the businessman says,
"When I say the church should be run like a business, I don't mean that we look only at the bottom line of the budget. I mean that we should take a lot of the ego and emotions out and stay focused on the 'bottom line' of the church—doing God's will. That way, it's not about personal worries and needs and all that. We remember that there is something more important than the fact that we can't agree on the color of the new carpet."

4.3 Healthy congregations expect faithful pastors . . .
to pursue holiness.

"Prayer, Bible study, and watching good people—these give me some idea of what it means to be holy."[7]

—a United Methodist pastor

IN GALATIANS 5:22-23, Paul identifies the fruit of the Spirit: "love, joy, peace, patience, kindness, generosity, faithfulness, gentleness, and self-control." Together, these qualities describe a special kind of life—indeed, a life that could be called "holy." In contemporary terms, when Christians think of people who are "holy," they may well imagine people who have their priorities straight, people who are not worried about advancing their own egos, people who exude a kind of calming wisdom. These steady disciples never appear to be anxious and are often quite joyful. They are comfortable conversing with God; indeed, more of their prayer time is spent listening than speaking. Their strong sense of self is grounded in their willingness to practice self-sacrifice and self-denial in order to be transformed into a more Christ-like person.

Such individuals make a difference to those around them. As a friend of mine, a Roman Catholic layperson, once put it to me, "People need to have a holy person in their lives."[8] She believed very strongly that everyone benefited from being around someone who could help put a crisis into perspective or who could discern God's presence in surprising ways. All Christians are called to be holy, and most churches have laypeople whose piety is a gift to everyone in their communities.

Pastors are to help their churches be a "royal priesthood, a holy nation, God's own people," called to proclaim God's mighty acts (1 Peter 2:9). Indeed, in *ordination*, the church sets pastors apart to do just this, providing for their material welfare so that they do not need to worry about what they will eat or what clothes they will wear.

Pastors do not need to be the holiest person in the congregation. (Indeed, many pastors and laypeople will tell you that this is highly unlikely!) But they do need to pursue lives of joyful obedience and to encourage their church members to do likewise. The pastor leads the people in a common journey of *walking with* God

Ann the young pastor says,
"I loved when a church member asked me, 'What does it mean to be holy?' He was not asking a theoretical question—he really wanted to know. He wasn't afraid of the word. I think a lot of us are. He was asking 'What is truly important?' That's a beautiful question."

Rita the spiritual director says,
"The qualities we associate with holiness require careful cultivation, and such cultivation takes time. If a church truly wants a pastor who pursues holiness, the lay leaders need to work with the pastor to make sure she prioritizes time for reading the Bible, prayer, and contemplation. An hour spent in silence, listening for God's voice or simply soaking up God's loving presence, will be more valuable than an hour spent reviewing the budget."

Bill the senior pastor says,
"Pastors who have difficulties making time for Scripture and listening to God in prayer need to remember that their own commitment to growing as a mature, wise, calming, indeed holy disciples is one of the things their people need the most."

in such a way that people grow *closer to* God. Holiness is a gift from God, but, as with all such gifts, God expects us to respond faithfully and diligently.

Faithful pastors pursue this call to be holy as the Lord is holy without becoming "holier than thou." (Indeed, humility born of the awareness of one's sinfulness is a trait of holy people.) And just like everyone else, pastors face challenges, temptations, and difficult times. Healthy congregations can provide the encouragement necessary for their pastors by letting them know that their commitment to holiness makes a difference to the entire church.

"Holiness" is not a private matter; it has a powerful social impact. One person's sincere piety can be leavening for an entire church.

At my church, this Expectation is:

__**Not** Discussed   __**Not** Practiced

__**Not Widely** Agreed Upon   __**Not Widely** Practiced

__**Somewhat** Agreed Upon   __**Somewhat** Practiced

__**Widely** Agreed Upon   __**Widely** Practiced

__**Not** Applicable   __**Not** Applicable

4.4 Healthy congregations expect faithful pastors . . .
to be learning and growing constantly.

"If the pastor does not seek out things that stretch the imagination, then how can the pastor lead others into something that stretches beyond themselves?"[9]

—a New Testament scholar

WE EXPECT DOCTORS TO continue learning more about medicine throughout their careers. We expect car mechanics to stay up to date on how to repair new cars. Indeed, part of our understanding of a professional is *professional* development.

Centuries ago, the monastic world had a phrase that might apply to pastors today: "the love of learning and the desire for God."[10] Constant study and the love of God belong together. The more we know about the Bible, the world, and people, the more we are amazed at the goodness, power, and love of God. At its best, the practices of learning—both from books and from other people—enhance our faith.

Monastic culture often encouraged learning, and some congregations today expect learned clergy. But not all churches encourage pastoral study. I teach a group of United Methodist pastors who are committed to a multi-year educational program through the beginning years of their ministries. I regularly hear from these pastor-students about well-meaning congregants who come up to them as they head off to school and say, "We don't want you to change." Fortunately, these men and women are dedicated to their studies because they want to change. As one of them said, with tears welling up, "I just want to be the best pastor I can be."

In addition to particular church cultures, another challenge facing professionals, including pastors, is that life-long learning requires a healthy combination of humility and self-confidence. Sometimes people have such a low opinion of themselves that they believe they are who they are and are never going to improve. Because the ego is so fragile, these individuals have a very difficult time with the hard work of self-reflection and personal development. At other times, people are so self-congratulatory (or so convinced God is already blessing everything they do) that they are unable to recognize the simple fact that there is indeed room for growth.

Ed the businessman says,

"I always ask my pastor what books or professional journals he is reading. If I make it clear that I value a pastor who values learning, I encourage him to dedicate the time and energy needed for professional development and, ultimately, more faithful service."

Dennis the bishop says,

"Many denominations require local churches to provide continuing-education time to pastors. This is a terrific practice—if the pastor takes advantage of it. All too often, pastors are reluctant to take time from their churches to attend a conference. The congregation as a whole, and lay leaders in particular, can gently remind the pastor that her continuing education is for their benefit."

Bill the senior pastor says,

"Pastoral study is not for impressing the congregation with fancy words (which many congregants do not appreciate anyway). The pastor's practices of study are ultimately for the people of God."

A faithful pastor is not afraid to learn. She welcomes constructive criticism. (See Expectation 8.3.) A faithful pastor combines diligent study from books with attentive listening to the congregation. To use the terminology from Expectation 4.2, a faithful pastor is sufficiently "differentiated" to remain detached enough to learn from difficult, even tense times in the church. A faithful pastor is always asking, "How can I learn from this moment? How can I do something differently next time to better serve the people of God?" This person is confident enough to remain humble and learn constantly. Hence, the saying, "leading requires learning."

The pastoral office is, in part, a teaching office. The best teachers never presume they already know everything there is to know. Faithful pastors integrate regular times for learning into their weekly and annual rhythms.

At my church, this Expectation is:

__**Not** Discussed   __**Not** Practiced

__**Not Widely** Agreed Upon   __**Not Widely** Practiced

__**Somewhat** Agreed Upon   __**Somewhat** Practiced

__**Widely** Agreed Upon   __**Widely** Practiced

__**Not** Applicable   __**Not** Applicable

4.5 Healthy congregations expect faithful pastors . . .
to be involved in a peer group for support, collaboration, and accountability.

"I fear we [pastors] have internalized the hallmark of our American culture—individualism."[11]

—Mahan Siler

ALTHOUGH THIS BOOK stresses *mutual ministry* and the importance of clergy and laity serving together, the pastor of a church does have a distinctive role. She remains set apart from the congregation (as per her *ordination*). Unfortunately, it is easy for her to be too far apart.

Pastor and author Mahan Siler has observed that pastoral ministry is "mostly offered by individuals in virtual isolation." This is in part because most pastors are solo pastors. But more fundamentally, many pastors consciously or unconsciously adopt an "overly individualized model." Although seminarians are warned against being Lone Ranger pastors, Siler notes that this kind of ministry has become the norm.[12]

It is hardly surprising that loneliness is common among pastors. (The importance of sustaining confidentiality further prevents pastors from discussing issues among their congregants with others.) Moreover, as Parker Palmer notes, "The growth of any craft depends on the shared practice and honest dialogue among the people who do it."[13] Pastors separated from colleagues (as most are) reduce their occasions for professional development. Lawyers learn from seeing peers at work, but pastors have relatively few such opportunities. Finally, pastors need other pastors for *accountability*. It is all too easy for pastors to avoid responsibilities they do not like—and a pastor struggling with an issue may not have a place of *safety* to reflect on his own patterns of behavior with peer guidance. Siler reminds his fellow clergy of something most of them already know deep down—that leading congregations by themselves "invites timidity, overfunctioning, hubris, and burnout."[14]

Siler himself has developed a program of collegial church communities called Anan Cara (soul friend) that addresses some of the challenges clergy regularly face. He notes that many clergy peer groups fail to thrive for a number of reasons: poor structure or lack of trust, a failure

Lisa the pharmacist says,
"Our pastor has a good colleague group. When something happens in the life of our church, we encourage him to process it with his fellow ministers. We know he is not 'gossiping' about us but is trying to find ways to improve the situation or improve himself."

Ed the businessman says,
"We include the pastor's participation in a peer group as part of the expectations of our Mutual Ministry Review process. If something frustrating is going on, we'd rather have him vent there than to take it out on the congregation. We learned the hard way that such things can happen."

Rita the spiritual director says,
"Jesus sent his apostles out in pairs, not by themselves. He understood that preaching the good news in a broken world was not going to be easy—even for those filled with the power of the Holy Spirit. I wish more pastors recognized the wisdom of our Lord's own example."

to commit the time needed, or hesitation to hold one another accountable. However, such gatherings, when done wisely, provide the support, collaboration, and *accountability* needed for promoting the self-knowledge and self-surrender required of faithful ministry. As the introduction to this chapter noted, pastoral *maturity* requires both enhancing the self and overcoming the self. Faithful collegial communities help make these possible.

Effective clergy groups take time—more than just a quick breakfast on the go. But pastors and congregants do well to appreciate how the pastor's time away from the congregation benefits the entire church.

At my church, this Expectation is:

__**Not** Discussed
__**Not Widely** Agreed Upon
__**Somewhat** Agreed Upon
__**Widely** Agreed Upon
__**Not** Applicable

__**Not** Practiced
__**Not Widely** Practiced
__**Somewhat** Practiced
__**Widely** Practiced
__**Not** Applicable

4.6 Healthy congregations expect faithful pastors . . .
to respect their bodies as temples of the Holy Spirit.

"I tend to put my work ahead of my health. . . . If I planned a day off, and [church members] call me, and there's a need, there I go."[15]

—a United Methodist pastor

PASTORS LEARN IN CHURCH history classes of all the controversies the church has faced about the body. Many ancient Greek philosophies saw the body as a kind of prison; their adherents believed the goal of the good life was to transcend the body's limitations altogether. Some Christian heretics believed Jesus could not have taken on flesh because flesh is corrupt and what is holy does not take on corruption. Paul does not help much when he writes, "To set the mind on the flesh is death, but to set the mind on the Spirit is life and peace" (Romans 8:6).

Against all these other ways of thinking about the human body, the church has consistently affirmed that the body is a gift from God; that Jesus really did become a person with human flesh; that he was resurrected bodily; and that we will "be united with him in a resurrection like his" (Romans 6:5). Paul himself calls us to account: "Do you not know that your body is a temple of the Holy Spirit within you?" (1 Corinthians 6:19). Given this, we might think pastors might be more likely than most to take good care of their bodies.

That is simply not the case; indeed, the opposite is true. The extensive research of Duke Divinity School's Clergy Health Initiative has confirmed what many have long suspected.[16] This program has demonstrated that, as a whole, pastors find their work to be so stressful and time consuming that their overall health suffers drastically. We should therefore not be surprised that "denominational health insurance agencies report that medical costs for clergy are higher than for any other professional group!"[17]

Pastors do not have good health practices for a number of reasons (many of which are discussed in this book!). Healthy churches expect faithful pastors to take good care of all the gifts they have received, including their bodies.

Lisa the pharmacist says,
"I like to invite my pastor to go for a walk together. We could both use the exercise! And we have a chance to get to know each other as people."

Rita the spiritual director says,
"One pastor spoke about feeling guilty about going to the gym during the day. What would members of the congregation say? He could not go 'after work,' since work often did not end until the close of the evening committee meeting. He wanted to be seen as a caring, giving, constantly working pastor, and he felt he needed 'permission' from the congregation to go to the gym. Healthy congregations might help their pastors by including a gym membership in their covenantal agreement—and by telling their pastors that they expect them to use it regularly."

Bill the senior pastor says,
"Pastors encourage church members to get annual check-ups, eat properly, and get some form of exercise. They can do the same for themselves. It's really not that hard. Just put these things on the calendar and do it."

Caring for one's own body is a very sensitive subject for many people—and pastors, like many others, may need help.

Pastors visit men and women in hospitals and see on a regular basis the diseases and difficulties that happen when people do not hold their bodies in high regard. Pastors might do well to learn from their experience of caring for others in order to care better for themselves.

At my church, this Expectation is:

__**Not** Discussed	__**Not** Practiced
__**Not Widely** Agreed Upon	__**Not Widely** Practiced
__**Somewhat** Agreed Upon	__**Somewhat** Practiced
__**Widely** Agreed Upon	__**Widely** Practiced
__**Not** Applicable	__**Not** Applicable

4.7 Healthy congregations expect faithful pastors . . .
to be able to receive care.

"It's our pride that gets in the way of letting others help us."[18]

—a Baptist minister

FOR MANY PEOPLE (particularly those in the caring professions), receiving care is not easy. Pastors see themselves as the fixers and helpers, not the people in need. Like many, perhaps most, Americans, they value independence and self-reliance, preferring the heroic, silent, even stoic struggle as opposed to asking for help. Indeed, at its worst, the helpers sometimes *need* those who appear to need them, since having someone else to help makes people feel better about themselves.

Congregations sometimes reinforce such unstated assumptions about virtuous behavior. When I was a hospital chaplain, one pastor spoke to me angrily about his congregation not tolerating the fact that he was genuinely sick and in pain. He had been told simply that, especially because he was a pastor, "You should have more faith." From their point of view, his faith should be strong enough to see him through physical pain. For some churches, it is important that the pastor not be seen to have any issues. Since Christians sometimes project their own spiritual desires onto the pastor (see Expectation 10.4), the pastor—as the embodiment of what righteous faith can bring—may be expected to be free of any personal problems.

In their preaching, teaching, and pastoral care, pastors often struggle against these personal and communal expectations. They present to the congregation a biblical vision of a community of care. They preach on biblical passages about caring for widows and orphans or imitating Jesus' ministry of healing or visiting the sick. Pastors know that helping those in need is fundamental to the mission of a church and to the lives of individual Christians. Pastors form their churches to be communities of care. But the question remains: Are pastors able to receive care themselves?

Healthy congregations expect their pastors, as faithful Christians, to model their lives on Jesus. Jesus received care—and honored the caregivers. He was dependent on his mother for milk and warmth; he welcomed the

Lisa the pharmacist says,
"I remember a pastor who developed a number of health issues. Over the course of a few years, he could no longer help at the food bank, participate in work days, or even get up the stairs very easily. What struck me was how gracious he was about it. He was giving up things he cared about, and he didn't let his pride get in the way. He didn't mind when folks helped him up the stairs or moved things around for him. I hope I can learn to be that gracious when I get older."

Ed the businessman says,
"I turned the tables on our pastor once—I told him if he didn't let us help him when his basement flooded, I wasn't going to listen to any more of his sermons on helping others."

Bill the senior pastor says,
"I remember one time when I had minor surgery. At first, I tried to tell church members that we didn't need any food brought by. We really did have plenty! But I realized they wanted to care for me like anyone else. I was surprised by how much that made me feel like part of the church. After receiving such abundant love, my wife paraphrased the twenty-third Psalm: 'My casserole dish overflows.'"

anointing of his feet; and like a nursing home patient with parched lips, he thirsted desperately. We are all vulnerable—literally woundable, like Christ on the cross—and so we all need care at times in our lives.

Silent, stoic endurance may be a cultural value, but Jesus' calling out from the cross is the more faithful model for those in need of care.

At my church, this Expectation is:

__**Not** Discussed	__**Not** Practiced
__**Not Widely** Agreed Upon	__**Not Widely** Practiced
__**Somewhat** Agreed Upon	__**Somewhat** Practiced
__**Widely** Agreed Upon	__**Widely** Practiced
__**Not** Applicable	__**Not** Applicable

4.8 Healthy congregations expect faithful pastors . . .

to honor their own families just as pastors encourage church members to honor theirs.

"Clergy families are under unique stresses. [People] expect us to have a perfect marriage. And many of us . . . have marriages that are hanging by a thread."[19]

—a United Methodist pastor

PASTORS PROVIDE marriage counseling to those about to get married as well as to those who are struggling with their families. They give advice on what makes for healthy, thriving family relationships that are vital witnesses to the goodness of God. But, as with so many other topics in this chapter, the question is: Do pastors follow their own advice? Pastors ask congregants to attend to the needs of their marriages. Do pastors who are married devote attention to their own marriages? Whether married or not, do pastors nurture their relationships with other family members and with long-term friends?

The life of a pastor presents a number of distinctive problems for families (in addition to the common challenges facing every family). Many, perhaps most, church meetings take place in the evening, when the pastor could be with her family. A pastor can get an emergency call at any time (and pastors can get calls that aren't emergencies at any time). Pastors absorb a great deal of sorrow and brokenness from the lives of congregants; yet they need to be in a healthy frame of mind to support their own families. Pastors want to be open and available to the congregation and its needs, but doing so can make family life unpredictable.

Further, a church may be a very good place for a pastor, but it may not be a good place for the pastor's family (in terms of, for example, personal relationships, age-appropriate programs, and worship style). Pastors sometimes work so hard to please the congregation that they come home exhausted, and home becomes a place to blow off steam. The pastor may be so concerned about avoiding conflict or tension in the church that he represses frustrations, frustrations that get taken out on his family.

Bill the senior pastor says,
"Whenever my congregants tell me to stop cleaning the fellowship hall after a meal and go home to my family, I know that's a good sign. It means they believe I am already doing 'enough' in the life of the church. And it means they care about us as people."

Ann the young pastor says,
"I don't want my daughter thinking that 'church' is that place where Mommy always is when she is not at her soccer game. I hope I am never in a church that pits me against my family."

Dennis the bishop says,
"A friend of mine is always clear when he is discussing the possibility of coming to serve a church: he will not attend any church events or meetings on his family night. And he lives by this covenantal agreement. He models honoring the family, both for his own sake and for the sake of the congregation."

Chapter 1 discussed how the ability to set *boundaries* promotes both a healthy family life and a stronger congregation. *Boundaries* about time commitments and the agreed-upon expectations of the pastor provide much-needed stability for families, and send the signal that the pastor does in fact cherish her family. A pastor who sets good limits creates space for congregants to use their gifts for the church. Ultimately, as part of being in a *covenant*, the welfare of the pastor and her family is of fundamental concern to the church (see chapter 9).

Pastors and churches do well to remember that pastors are called to serve in a church for a season, not for life. By contrast, wedding vows are "until death do us part." God calls men and women to be pastors, but a pastoral vocation does not supersede one's calling as a spouse and parent.

At my church, this Expectation is:

__**Not** Discussed   __**Not** Practiced
__**Not Widely** Agreed Upon   __**Not Widely** Practiced
__**Somewhat** Agreed Upon   __**Somewhat** Practiced
__**Widely** Agreed Upon   __**Widely** Practiced
__**Not** Applicable   __**Not** Applicable

4.9 Healthy congregations expect faithful pastors . . .
to observe Sabbath rest.

"To act as if the world cannot get along without our work for one day in seven is a startling display of pride that denies the sufficiency of our generous Maker."[20]

—Dorothy C. Bass

SABBATH REST IS God's great gift. Although we are called to honest work most of the time, one day is to be set aside for resting in the goodness of God and reminding ourselves that we are not slaves to our work. In observing Sabbath we imitate God's own rest on the seventh day of creation. We all need Sabbath rest, pastors especially, since most are likely working six or seven days per week. In a recent survey, over half of pastors reported difficulties observing Sabbath.[21]

Not respecting God's call to put down our pens and ploughshares is a sign that at some fundamental level we think we need to be busy all the time—either because God needs us to help make things right or because we feel we need to prove our own self-worth. Since pastors are doing God's work, pastors are tempted to justify their disobeying God for God's own sake. The seemingly heroic pastor, an apparently faithful laborer in the field, may well be demonstrating a lack of trust in God. Instead of practicing the self-knowledge that Sabbath fosters (and which has been discussed throughout this chapter), the pastor ends up stoking her own ego and her own anxieties.

Healthy congregations expect their pastors to observe Sabbath. Putting aside their own egotistical needs to achieve (or to be seen by the congregation as a good pastor), these pastors can gratefully rest in the goodness of God. Instead of being anxious about the budget or not having visited someone, they experience a peaceful awareness of God's sufficiency. (See Expectation 4.3 on holiness.) Yes, there are things to be done, but the faithful pastor recognizes that many, perhaps most, things on the pastoral "to do" list are secondary to maintaining a trusting relationship with God. Good works flow from faith; works-righteousness hardly leads to a robust faith.

Rita the spiritual director says,
"God's gift of Sabbath is for everyone, clergy and laity alike. We are all overworked, over-stretched, over-stressed. God wants us to serve, yes, and to work hard, and even to pick up a cross and follow. But God also wants us to enjoy God's goodness. Jesus addresses disciples as friends, and we are all children of God. Children, not workers. When we rest in God's parental love, we draw closer to God through abiding trust, joyful leisure, and grateful reflection. We worry about not having enough time—but this is the time we need."

Lisa the pharmacist says,
"Our previous pastor often preached on the importance of keeping Sabbath. He worked seven days a week, and it always seemed a bit hypocritical for him to talk about Sabbath-keeping. I think what he meant by observing Sabbath was coming to church and doing things. That was part of our problem when he was here—church was never a place to rest."

Bill the senior pastor says,
"Choose a strategy for observing Sabbath. A pastor friend of mine observes the Jewish Sabbath and does no work from Friday night until Saturday night. That fits in well with her pastoral responsibilities on Sunday mornings. It also makes sure she and her family can enjoy a Friday night together without her having to go off somewhere."

As Dorothy C. Bass notes, quoting the Puritan Sabbath-keepers of old, "good Sabbaths make good Christians."[22]

At my church, this Expectation is:

__**Not** Discussed   __**Not** Practiced
__**Not Widely** Agreed Upon   __**Not Widely** Practiced
__**Somewhat** Agreed Upon   __**Somewhat** Practiced
__**Widely** Agreed Upon   __**Widely** Practiced
__**Not** Applicable   __**Not** Applicable

Questions for You and Your Church

- What does *holiness* mean to you?
- Do you know someone who seems to be holy? How do you respond to that person?
- In what ways does your pastor strike you as a holy person?
- On a scale of 1–10, with 1 being highly anxious, and 10 being very calm, where would you rate yourself? Your pastor? Your church as a whole?
- What do you want your pastor to learn more about?
- As you think about your own life as a Christian and church member, what would you like to learn more about? Would you like your pastor to help you?
- How would you assess what you know of your pastor's practices of self-care or continuing education?
- How would you complete the sentence "Our pastor would be healthier if . . ."?

5

Healthy Servant Leadership
SERVING SO OTHERS CAN LEAD

Chapter 3 emphasized that there are many temptations to focus not on God's activity but on the pastor's. This chapter similarly stresses the importance of focusing not on the pastor's work, but on the congregation's. Taken together, these chapters orient the church toward *God's* activity and the *congregation's* response as shepherded by the *pastor* (note the order!).

Pastors are called to model their ministry after the example of Jesus, who came "not to be served but to serve" (Mark 10:45). They follow the Good Shepherd who risks his life for the sheep. In their role as shepherds, pastors lead, but they do so for the sake of the flock under their care. Therefore they are called to be servant-leaders, simultaneously humble and exalted. Although people look up to them, they focus the people's gaze beyond themselves to God and to God's work among the people.[1]

At its best, the pastor's leadership prompts the free and joyful response of the community of faith in worship and mission. The foundational principles of *ordination, covenant,* and *mutual ministry* described in chapter 1 are all clearly evident. Unfortunately, if a pastor does not maintain the *eustress* inherent in servant leadership—if a pastor is either too servile or too domineering—everyone suffers.

This chapter addresses the dangers of pastors (1) needing to be liked by the congregation, and (2) needing to be in control. Faithful pastors have needs, but they also have the personal strength and congregational support to lead so others can serve—and to serve so others can lead.

Healthy congregations expect faithful pastors . . .
5.1 – to be preparing the congregation for their eventual successors.
5.2 – not to overfunction such that the congregation starts to underfunction.
5.3 – to empower other leaders in the church.
5.4 – to take a sabbatical and let the congregation take a sabbatical too.
5.5 – to honor both silence and speech.
5.6 – to make mistakes, to disappoint, and to practice forgiveness.
5.7 – not to be too proud or insecure to ask for help.

5.1 Healthy congregations expect faithful pastors . . .
to be preparing the congregation for their eventual successors.

"As a pastor, one of your most important jobs is to set expectations for your successors. If your primary goal is to be liked, what are you doing for those who come after you?"[2]

—a preaching professor and former pastor

THE RELATIONSHIP BETWEEN a pastor and congregation is intense, rich, and meaningful. But it is also temporary. This is an inherent aspect of *ordination*, being set apart.

Faithful pastors honor the work of their predecessors—and they appreciate it when the congregation receives them without constantly making comparisons or carrying rigid expectations for what the pastor is supposed to be. No one likes looking over her shoulder to find the ghost of a predecessor.

Pastors should also look ahead to the next person who will occupy their pulpit. How can a pastor shepherd a church in such a way that her successor comes into a healthier church? How can a pastor serve as a leader so that the church can thrive in a covenantal relationship without being overly dependent on the pastor? (See co-dependency in Expectation 10.5.) These questions are crucial because they help the pastor focus less on his own need to be liked or to be in charge and more on the long-term needs of the congregation. By considering his successor, the pastor is freed from needing immediate results and can advocate for what is in the church's long-term best interests. It helps prioritize ministry needs and allows a pastor who recognizes a problem to address it gently without anxiety-creating haste.

Such a focus encourages the congregation to think ahead, too, to put aside the natural fear of change and imagine how the church could develop. It fosters responsibility in the laity since they know the pastor won't be there forever. It reminds everyone that being in a church is a long-term proposition about a long-term relationship with God; "immediate results" are not necessary.

Faithful pastors are liberated to serve and lead congregations by keeping the future in mind—a future in which someone else will serve as pastor.

Lisa the pharmacist says,
"I try to be friendly with our customers, to remember their prescription histories, and to be ready to help them out. But I also want everyone at the pharmacy to be able to help each person. I owe it to the other staff members—and to future pharmacists—to keep my focus on the patient and the medicine, not on my own desires to be the pharmacist they depend on."

Ann the young pastor says,
"My predecessor at my first church was a supply preacher. He very publicly used to put his check in the offering plate each week as a sign of gratitude toward God and a sign of his offering his whole life to God. That would have been fine as a private devotion. But when I arrived, the church naturally expected me to do the same thing. I was viewed as being less righteous, less of a 'real' pastor, for actually needing money. That was not fair to me, and it was not fair to the church's understanding of its own responsibilities to support its pastor."

At my church, this Expectation is:

    __**Not** Discussed
    __**Not Widely** Agreed Upon
    __**Somewhat** Agreed Upon
    __**Widely** Agreed Upon
    __**Not** Applicable

    __**Not** Practiced
    __**Not Widely** Practiced
    __**Somewhat** Practiced
    __**Widely** Practiced
    __**Not** Applicable

Dennis the bishop says,
"I often have to comfort the clergy I shepherd by reminding them that the important changes in a congregation they work so hard for will lead to a better church. They may never get to enjoy that church, but their successor will. They need to understand that this is part of the call to ordained ministry. Hopefully, they will also get to 'inherit' a healthy church."

5.2 Healthy congregations expect faithful pastors . . .
not to overfunction such that the congregation starts to underfunction.

"When I decide whether to do something or to ask someone else to do it, the question I must ask is: How will my doing this help the church?"[3]

—a Presbyterian pastor

THREE POWERFUL FORCES come together that lead pastors to do more in the church than they should.

Theologically, Jesus' own emphasis on unhesitating service is a crucial model. *Institutionally*, pastors depend on engaged, energetic people who are willing to volunteer. Won't people volunteer more if the pastor is setting an example by doing more? (This problem is reinforced by the absence of a clear job description with specific *boundaries*; see chapter 7.) *Personally*, the pastor, like most people, probably enjoys being liked. Won't people like him more if he takes care of things for them?

All of these can combine in such a way that the pastor overfunctions—does more than she should be doing—in the life of a church. The pastor steps in where others hesitate; she prepares the budget, teaches Sunday school, and makes sure that everyone gets a birthday card. This seems like Christ-like service. This helps the institution get things done. And it encourages people to like the pastor. These theological, institutional, and personal forces are powerful, but they are temptations that must be resisted lest the entire church be set up for failure.

Not only is this draining on the pastor's physical, mental, and spiritual health, but it also restricts the life of the congregation. Congregations underfunction—do less than they could be doing in response to the gospel—either because they can "get away" with doing less or because the pastor's behavior inhibits the members' actions. The pastor may not be the only person overfunctioning: the 80–20 rule, which says that 20 percent of the people do 80 percent of the work, often takes effect when a few people in the congregation join the pastor in overfunctioning.

Lisa the pharmacist says,
"I appreciate it when the pastor helps clean up the kitchen after a fellowship meal every now and then. There's something to doing chores together and chatting. But I'd rather my pastor know that he doesn't have to cook the meal, too. Didn't the office of deacon arise so that pastors could focus on what they are supposed to focus on—Scripture and prayer?"

Ann the young pastor says,
"It is so hard to say no. Someone calls and asks you to do something, and it seems like it will build goodwill. I have to tell myself over and over again to respond to requests and ideas by encouraging others to take responsibility. My 'no' can be an opportunity for someone else's 'yes.'"

Dennis the bishop says,
"It's better for the church to have to wrestle with the lack of volunteers than for the pastor to be doing so many things. It only gets worse over time, because the congregation never has to assume its own responsibilities. And when the people don't follow the energetic example of the pastor, the pastor is tempted to do even more to encourage others to do something. People would be surprised by how much trying to 'lead by example' stresses leaders out."

The principles of *ordination, covenant,* and *boundaries* discussed in chapter 1 address the problem of overfunctioning by articulating a healthy vision of pastoral-congregational *mutual ministry.* Indeed, this is the subject of the entire book.

Proper servant leadership is a sign of faith—a sign of trusting in God and a sign of trusting in the laity. Congregations promote healthy pastoral functioning by providing adequate staff and volunteers for the work of the church (or by agreeing that they will have to cease doing some things).

At my church, this Expectation is:

__**Not** Discussed   __**Not** Practiced
__**Not Widely** Agreed Upon   __**Not Widely** Practiced
__**Somewhat** Agreed Upon   __**Somewhat** Practiced
__**Widely** Agreed Upon   __**Widely** Practiced
__**Not** Applicable   __**Not** Applicable

5.3 Healthy congregations expect faithful pastors . . .
to empower other leaders in the church.

"If you want to be a good leader, don't care if you get the credit!"[4]

—a retired Presbyterian pastor

WHEN I ASKED PASTORS what their greatest joy in ministry is, pastors typically responded by saying something like "helping others become better disciples." As shepherds, pastors nurture their flocks. They love thanking people for their service, showing gratitude on behalf of the congregation, and encouraging others to share their time and talents.

Sometimes, however, things get in the way. Pastors may feel pressure to be efficient, or they may not trust certain people to complete a task properly. They may feel concerned about overstretched, weary lay leaders who would also benefit from better *boundaries*. Sometimes a pastor simply feels it would be quicker to prepare the budget statement herself than to develop the skills of the treasurer. And sometimes pastors don't recognize their own need to be in control.

Despite these many "reasons" a pastor might have for not taking the time to nurture others, helping congregants respond to Jesus' call in their lives is a primary pastoral responsibility. Christians need pastors to guide, strengthen, and prepare them for lives of grateful obedience. We all feel intense joy when we know we are doing God's work—even if visiting a nursing home is challenging. Indeed, we sense that we are restored to a beautiful fellowship with God when we recognize we are cooperating with God's will.

Furthermore, one way we grow as Christians is by trying to serve and failing, from learning from our mistakes. Pastors do have a buck-stops-here responsibility for leading an institution, but sometimes servant leadership requires allowing mistakes to happen—mistakes that can then lead not just to better institutional functioning but also, and more importantly, to church members who are better disciples of Jesus.

Faithful pastors remember that one of their priorities is "to equip the saints [their own church members!] for the work of ministry, for building up of the body of Christ" (Ephesians 4:12).

Ed the businessman says,

"All too often, church people are asked to do things they simply are not called to do. Just because a pastor wants them to do it, it does not mean God is calling them to do it. A pastor who is a good shepherd will help people identify where their heart truly is, where his passion is, and match that with the needs of the church and the church's mission. That's when laypeople can serve with faith and energy even in the most trying circumstances."

Bill the senior pastor says,

"Seeing someone grow in confidence and ability—now, that is exciting! I don't need to be the one making presentations or leading prayers before meals. Ministry is about teaching, and like a teacher, I take my greatest pleasure from watching someone learn to do something new."

Rita the spiritual director says,

"A mother can either prepare the vegetables herself or teach her child to learn how to use a paring knife. It takes more time and patience to do the latter, but in the long run, it is necessary—both for the mother and for the child."

At my church, this Expectation is:

__**Not** Discussed

__**Not Widely** Agreed Upon

__**Somewhat** Agreed Upon

__**Widely** Agreed Upon

__**Not** Applicable

__**Not** Practiced

__**Not Widely** Practiced

__**Somewhat** Practiced

__**Widely** Practiced

__**Not** Applicable

5.4 Healthy congregations expect faithful pastors . . .
to take a sabbatical and let the congregation take a sabbatical too.

"It was hard for me to step back for a season, but the sabbatical helped me and the congregation become a better church."[5]

—a Baptist pastor

BASED ON THE BIBLICAL concepts of ceasing from labor one day a week or one year in seven (see Leviticus 25), a pastoral sabbatical is a time of stepping back from the immediate demands of pastoral ministry. Typically for two months or more, a pastor will enter into an intentional program of continuing education and spiritual refreshment, often at a seminary or other theological center. Pastors benefit from this time away from the congregation—during a sabbatical they learn from other preachers and worship leaders; they have time to study Scripture or a particular facet of ministry in greater depth; and they return to their congregations with more energy. Many denominations strongly encourage or even require that congregations provide a sabbatical for their pastors.

But just as there are always many good excuses for not taking a day off, there are always many good excuses for not taking a sabbatical.

As noted in other sections of this chapter, pastors may be hesitant to request or take a sabbatical for a number of personal reasons, including their need to be needed by the congregation or the reluctance to let someone else lead "their" church. Often, the stated institutional concerns—"the church is entering into a critical period in its life!"—may be masking these personal needs.

Faithful pastors trust in God and in the congregation, and are able to receive a sabbatical as part of God's guidance of their covenantal life together. The fact that the leader can step away signals trust and a confidence that the church does not need to worry about a lack of leadership.

Congregations, too, benefit from a sabbatical. They get to hear a different preacher and have opportunities for reviewing what they need to be doing

Ed the businessman says,

"I've seen too many employees in too many companies start dragging because they are exhausted and have lost their sense of purpose. Vacations are great, but these people could use sabbaticals—times to reorient or recommit. In many ways, pastors are no different from many other folks; it's just that for pastors and academics, the idea of a sabbatical is already acceptable."

Dennis the bishop says,

"I am always ready to recommend the idea of sabbatical for my churches. Sometimes giving the pastor a few months away is the best way to refresh the minister and give her a chance to recover a sense of hopefulness for the church. People come to church in part to relieve their own stresses and worries. The last thing a stressed-out people need is a stressed-out pastor."

Rita the spiritual director says,

"I see many pastors who are simply exhausted. Sometimes, they don't maintain good boundaries. Sometimes, there is simply so much going on in the life of the church. The ones I'm worried about, however, are the ones who resist the idea of a sabbatical. I see it as a real risk to the pastor and to the church when the pastor believes the church can't do without him for any period of time."

in their own church (or perhaps even reclaiming their roles). When an engaged, energetic pastor steps back for a season, the church has to remember how to thrive in her absence. When the pastor returns refreshed with new possibilities, she finds a church recommitted to its own life.

Congregations benefit enormously by having a pastor who has not grown "weary in doing what is right" (Galatians 6:9); they benefit from having a pastor who has had time for reading, reflection, and sustained prayer. Sabbaticals are a gift from God for both pastors and congregations.

At my church, this Expectation is:

__**Not** Discussed	__**Not** Practiced
__**Not Widely** Agreed Upon	__**Not Widely** Practiced
__**Somewhat** Agreed Upon	__**Somewhat** Practiced
__**Widely** Agreed Upon	__**Widely** Practiced
__**Not** Applicable	__**Not** Applicable

5.5 Healthy congregations expect faithful pastors . . .
to honor both silence and speech.

"Our new priest is really good at listening. You can tell by the way he speaks."[6]

—an Episcopal layperson

ONE OF THE ESSENTIAL GIFTS of servant leadership is discerning when to be silent and when to speak.

Sometimes, silence is called for—to preserve confidentiality; to listen for the Spirit while preparing sermons; to create room for others in the church to speak; to practice stillness; or to model listening for the congregation.

At other times, the pastor needs to speak—to guide the flow of congregational information; to bear prophetic witness; to moderate a meeting; to talk directly with people about difficult subjects (see, for example, avoiding triangulation, Expectation 10.2); or to confront problems in the church.

It would seem that the servant's role is to listen while the leader speaks—but it is often the other way around. Servants also need to speak out, and leaders also need to listen. The servant talks not from her own selfish desires but according to the will of the One who sent her. And the leader's listening is a sign that she values others as people, not as a means to an end.

Knowing whether a given moment is a time for speech or a time for silence is a great gift that a pastor can bring. Pastors who are aware of their own tendencies are able to recognize, for example, that their conflict-avoiding inclinations (or combative habits!) are not helping the church. Faithful pastors discern both themselves and the situation; they recognize when their personal inclinations to speech or silence are a strength or a hindrance.

When a pastor speaks, people listen. Or, perhaps more accurately, when a respected pastor speaks, people listen. Pastors earn this respect by remembering that "for everything there is a season . . . a time to keep silence, and a time to speak" (Ecclesiastes 3:1, 7).

Lisa the pharmacist says,
"I tell folks how medicines work, but I find that sometimes hearing people tell me why they need the medicine is just as important for their healing. People have stories, and listening respectfully is so powerful. Hurting people need to be heard by someone they can trust."

Ed the businessman says,
"Good communications in a church are hard to achieve. Sometimes there can be so much information, almost too much information, that needs to be conveyed effectively. When is the fellowship dinner? Who is revising the phone tree? Should a person be added to the prayer list? Was a decision ever reached about the repair projects? When people feel well informed, they are happier, but sometimes it takes repeating things over and over and over again before the information sticks in a person's head. Sometimes pastors think that if they put something in the bulletin once everyone has gotten the information."

Rita the spiritual director says,
"Self-control requires self-awareness. Many people in a church feel their lives are out of control, and what they need most in a pastor is a person who can practice self-discipline. So many people have been hurt by thoughtless words—words of anger, incivility, or even nervousness. By contrast, thought-filled words—words born of the discipline of listening, reflection, and prayer—can heal."

At my church, this Expectation is:

__**Not** Discussed

__**Not Widely** Agreed Upon

__**Somewhat** Agreed Upon

__**Widely** Agreed Upon

__**Not** Applicable

__**Not** Practiced

__**Not Widely** Practiced

__**Somewhat** Practiced

__**Widely** Practiced

__**Not** Applicable

5.6 Healthy congregations expect faithful pastors . . .
to make mistakes, to disappoint, and to practice forgiveness.

"The biggest issue to me is not getting defensive. We all make mistakes, but no one likes it when someone tries to make excuses or blame others. As a church, we should be able to handle failure better than anyone else."[7]

—a Lutheran layperson

ONE OF THE CHIEF PROBLEMS facing many, perhaps most, people in a church is what to do with personal mistakes. Some people are paralyzed by guilt or shame. Others are afraid to take risks for fear of failure. Still others have been badly wounded and wrestle with anger or self-doubt.

For their part, pastors may or may not actually enjoy being held to a higher standard. But because they so often feel that people look up to them and expect great things, they want to get everything right. They don't like the idea of letting people down, so they may have a hard time admitting mistakes or inadequacies.

But the ability of the pastor to demonstrate healthy ways of addressing his personal shortcomings can be a great gift to the congregation. Paul almost seems to rejoice in how his failures lead to the manifesting of God's grace. (See, for example, 1 Timothy 1:15.) His personal confession is grounded in a central theological conviction about the redemption of humanity through the death and resurrection of Jesus Christ.

Admitting mistakes and accepting our limitations is one way in which faithful pastors "practice *resurrection*." They realize that the ongoing process of dying and rising with Christ is a dynamic of sin, forgiveness, and new life. They recognize that in admitting their mistakes, they are being transformed and renewed —and they are providing an example for their congregants to do the same. They are not afraid of *accountability*, and this helps them hold others accountable, too.

Faithful pastors preach God's call to righteousness and set high standards for personal conduct. But trusting in the power of God's forgiveness, they also accept the inevitability of sin without being overcome

Rita the spiritual director says,
"I sometimes think the most important part of a worship service is the Confession of Sin and Declaration of Forgiveness. Sometimes it takes years of going to church and hearing the good news of forgiveness over and over, many, many times, before people can truly receive God's love into their hearts. The barriers, the doubts, the guilt—these can be overwhelming. And I wonder if pastors understand that God is just as eager to forgive them as to forgive the members of the congregation."

Ed the businessman says,
"I don't want my pastor to be perfect. She won't succeed. And she'll be so upset with herself that she will make it hard for the congregation. I want my pastor to do her best, to learn from her mistakes, and, when necessary, to ask for forgiveness."

Bill the senior pastor says,
"I don't like to eat crow, but when I'm wrong, I need to apologize as soon as possible. When pastors practice the 'fine art' of self-justification, this encourages everyone else to do the same. But when a pastor admits mistakes, this liberates others to do the same."

by it. As Paul declares, "There is therefore now no condemnation for those who are in Christ Jesus. For the law of the Spirit of life in Christ Jesus has set you free from the law of sin and of death" (Romans 8:1–2).

At my church, this Expectation is:

__**Not** Discussed   __**Not** Practiced

__**Not Widely** Agreed Upon   __**Not Widely** Practiced

__**Somewhat** Agreed Upon   __**Somewhat** Practiced

__**Widely** Agreed Upon   __**Widely** Practiced

__**Not** Applicable   __**Not** Applicable

5.7 Healthy congregations expect faithful pastors . . .
not to be too proud or insecure to ask for help.

"How can my congregation provide me any support if I don't let them know where I need the help?"[8]

—a United Methodist pastor

MANY PEOPLE DON'T LIKE to ask for help—and pastors are no exception.

As noted in the previous section, pastors don't want to let people down. They want to live into the people's high expectations. They want to be able to do it all, even if they really are not very good at, say, financial management, organization, or preaching. Further, it sometimes seems more efficient for the pastor to do things on his own, even when it comes to minor building repairs. Getting someone else involved requires several phone calls and several explanations of what is wrong. By the time that's all been done, the pastor could have completed the repair.

And in pastors, this very understandable human tendency can be a problem for the entire community. Whether it is asking for help with a properly pastoral skill (like preaching) or getting things done in the church (plumbing repairs), pastors need to remember why they are serving as pastors in the first place. (See *ordination, mutual ministry,* and *boundaries* in chapter 1.) They have a responsibility for developing their pastoral abilities, even if it would seem "embarrassing" to ask for constructive criticism of their preaching (see Expectation 8.3). They have a responsibility to respect the experience and insight of other members of the church.

Pastors who ask for help encourage others to shine. And pastors who accept help gratefully become better pastors.

Bill the senior pastor says,
"It can be embarrassing when you don't know the answer to a question about the Bible or when everyone realizes you don't understand the financial details of something. But if I admit my limitations and ask others for help, I find that it builds trust and develops relationships."

Lisa the pharmacist says,
"We had a pastor once who came to our lay leaders and asked that money be added to the budget for a consultant to help him improve his management style. It wasn't like we weren't aware of the problems, so the fact that he came to us first was refreshing. We moved the money around in the budget and made it work."

Dennis the bishop says,
"Lone Rangers. We call them Lone Rangers—pastors who think they can do it all without asking others for help. Having seen how restrictive—or even harmful—this can be for a church, I think there's a reason why the Lone Ranger never stays in one place for long."

At my church, this Expectation is:

__**Not** Discussed	__**Not** Practiced
__**Not Widely** Agreed Upon	__**Not Widely** Practiced
__**Somewhat** Agreed Upon	__**Somewhat** Practiced
__**Widely** Agreed Upon	__**Widely** Practiced
__**Not** Applicable	__**Not** Applicable

Questions for You and Your Church

- Does your pastor seem like he or she is more of a servant, a leader, or a servant-leader?
- What do your congregation and pastor need to do together in order for the pastor to have the right balance of servant and leader?
- Is the pastor overfunctioning? If so, how can the congregation help?
- How might the lay leaders in your congregation feel encouraged? Restricted?
- Does the pastor feel he needs to "do everything"? If so, is this more because of who he is or because the congregation is not providing enough staff and volunteer support—or both?
- How is the pastor serving as a model in asking for forgiveness?
- How comfortable is your pastor in asking for help?
- How would you complete this sentence: "In my opinion, the pastor and the lay leaders need to talk more about . . ."?
- How would you complete this sentence: "In my opinion, the pastor and the congregation as a whole need to talk more about . . ."?

Part III

What Faithful Pastors Expect from Healthy Congregations

Introduction

HOW TO CULTIVATE A GREAT PASTOR

Churches want their pastors to thrive. But do congregants know how to put pastors in a position to succeed? Or is it the case that through unintentional neglect, churches all too easily end up with patterns of behavior that make it harder for everyone?

To get a glimpse of how congregations can nurture great pastors, we can first look at the opposite: how congregations can exhibit certain behaviors that are harmful to pastors and, ultimately, to themselves. No church sets out intending to put the pastor in a position to fail. But hypothetically speaking, if a group of hypothetically annoying people were to set out and TRY to put a hypothetical person in a position to fail at a hypothetical job, they would probably want to:

- have a vague, open-ended job description—or, better still, have multiple job descriptions
- allow members of the organization to call anytime, day or night
- provide neither constructive criticism nor regular words of appreciation
- provide low wages relative to the amount of education required for the position
- allow hurtful speech toward her to go unchallenged
- try to control her personal behavior, including the behavior of her family
- discourage professional development and continuing education
- discourage personal *boundaries* and make it clear that the job comes before personal needs
- practice triangulation, pitting one person against another
- play the blame game and provide no mechanism for *accountability* for anyone else in the organization except her
- set unrealistic expectations, including the expectation that she will do all the work in the organization
- have a defeatist attitude toward the future of the organization

It is hard to imagine anyone succeeding under these kinds of "hypothetical" conditions. Indeed, depending on the circumstances, the presence of even just a few of these could make success very difficult. Yet these are what pastors sometimes face.

Many laypeople, too, are frustrated by these kinds of working conditions in their own professional lives, and they are helpless to change them. But a church community gets to set its own standards and practices for those who serve there.

Part III describes what faithful pastors expect from healthy congregations—what congregations can do to help put a pastor in a position to succeed. Put another way, these expectations make it possible for a congregation to cultivate a great pastor so that everyone can thrive together in a healthy *covenant*. Pastors arrive at churches equipped to serve; with the support of healthy congregations, they can develop into even better pastors.

If a church were to set out to put the pastor in a position to succeed—indeed, to thrive—what would it be sure to do? Chapters 6–10 set out to answer this question.

6

Mission and Ministry
FOLLOWING A CRUCIFIED SAVIOR AND BEING PREPARED TO DIE

This chapter draws primarily on three of the ten principles for a vibrant faith community: *purpose*, *eustress*, and *resurrection*.

Most churches have mission statements, but do these formal statements give a true sense of *purpose* that guides the decision-making and common life of the community? The first chapter of part II, "Theology and Worship," stressed the importance of focusing on God's activity; similarly, this first chapter of part III emphasizes constantly attending to God's call for a church and its people.

Pastoral leadership involves tension—the tension between where a congregation is and where God is calling it to go. Part of the pastor's role is to guide the people in seeking God's will. But, as many stories of the Bible indicate, this is not always easy or pleasing to the people of God. Hence, the inherent tension—the *eustress*—of church leadership is a crucial part of the mission and ministry of a congregation.

Finally, clarity about a church's future is required. Although there are churches that have many years ahead, numerous other churches are dying. Christians need not fear death. *Resurrection* applies both to people and communities. A Christian who accepts that she is dying can choose to live faithfully and continue to be a witness. So, too, can churches continue to thrive. Indeed, for both people and churches, it is often the acceptance of mortality that allows life to flourish.

Faithful pastors expect healthy congregations . . .
6.1 – to serve God above all and, thereby, to meet the people's deepest needs.
6.2 – to be clear about the church's current *purpose.*
6.3 – to believe that churches are called not to survive but to thrive.
6.4 – to trust that money follows mission.
6.5 – to take risks for the sake of the gospel.
6.6 – to recognize that all church members are called to lives of holy service.
6.7 – to let the pastor be a pastor.

6.1 Faithful pastors expect healthy congregations . . .
to serve God above all and, thereby, to meet the people's deepest needs.

"I'm not sure church is intended to be fun. I think it can be. It certainly won't be fun if we are always focused on 'what's in it for me.'"[1]

—John Richardson

JESUS SAYS, "Those who want to save their life will lose it, and those who lose their life for my sake will find it" (Matthew 16:25). True life is found through serving. A church that can offer meaningful service helps its members to find their lives.

But all too often, churches focus on addressing people's needs. After all, churches that want to attract new members (or simply hold on to existing ones) need to bring the people in somehow. As one pastor put it, "My greatest frustration in ministry . . . is people seeing the church as an institution designed to identify and meet their needs rather than the church calling, teaching, and empowering them to be disciples of Christ."[2] Author Elizabeth I. Steele identifies several consequences of this understandable approach to church life: a sense of entitlement among members, a regular source of disruption, and misplaced loyalties. She calls for a shift in our language and our thinking about what really matters in church life.[3]

If we reflect on our lives and ask about times we cherish, about times that truly satisfy, we will find that many of these memories are of times when we did something important, something God wanted us to do, and we did it well, perhaps even making significant sacrifices of time or money along the way. Perhaps we responded to a neighbor's fire. Perhaps we cared for a dying relative. Perhaps we served overseas, taking risks for something we believed in. We may also have fond memories of a favorite TV show or the victories of a favorite sports team, but memories of serving God and neighbor are memories of enduring meaning. They are what give us the greatest pride and, ultimately, joy and satisfaction.

Rita the spiritual director says,
"An incredible peace descends on the soul when a person decides to put God first. The same can happen in a congregation when the members recognize that the purpose of their church is not to satisfy their own wants."

Ed the businessman says,
"I don't want my church to consider me a consumer, someone whom the leaders need to keep happy at all costs. I want my church to help me see myself as a member of the body of Christ and to live into all that entails."

Bill the senior pastor says,
"As a pastor, I commit myself to serving God, and I know how much that can require. I expect my congregants to put God before their own wants. We have to remember that it is Christ's church, not ours, and on Sunday morning Christ is more interested in whether we welcomed people in his name than in whether we enjoyed the music."

Putting God first and serving God above all else entails sacrifice, to be certain, but such sacrifice can provide the satisfaction and meaning that sustains energy and commitment. Or not. Perhaps the problem facing many churches is that members do not experience their service to God and neighbor as truly meaningful and ultimately satisfying. They come to view helping prepare sacks of groceries at the food pantry as sheer drudgery. They may even see attending worship as a chore.

Pastors often experience the church as a community where they find the deepest fulfillment, and they want their members to feel the same way. Pastors know the truth of Augustine's famous prayer: "Restless is our heart until it comes to rest in thee."[4]

Paradoxically, it seems, churches can best address their members needs not by trying to keep the members "happy," but by giving them opportunities to respond in meaningful ways to what God is doing in their midst. Whether in the home, workplace, or church, there is a liberating quality to serving God and seeing our connection to a *purpose* much greater than our own desires. Meaningful sacrifice satisfies the soul.

Healthy churches help their members flourish by helping them fulfill the call to serve the living God in all aspects of their lives, including the congregation. This flourishing, in turn, provides an enduring foundation for sustaining the mission of the church.

At my church, this Expectation is:

__**Not** Discussed	__**Not** Practiced
__**Not Widely** Agreed Upon	__**Not Widely** Practiced
__**Somewhat** Agreed Upon	__**Somewhat** Practiced
__**Widely** Agreed Upon	__**Widely** Practiced
__**Not** Applicable	__**Not** Applicable

6.2 Faithful pastors expect healthy congregations . . .
to be clear about the church's current purpose.

"What would help the most in my church? Having a really frank discussion about who God is to them and what the church is supposed to do."[5]

—a United Methodist pastor

DO CHURCHES HAVE a clear sense of why they gather every Sunday, week in and week out? And do they have a firm sense of why they have a pastor instead of someone whose only task is to preach and lead worship once a week?

Some churches certainly do. One pastor reported with pride and gratitude, "I love my church. Everyone wants to be there. They know what they want to do—and they don't hesitate to tell me what they need from me." He acknowledged the squabbles. The church was not perfect. But he loved being there because they had a clear identity, as a small, family-friendly church in the inner city. And they had a definite commitment to three things: their music program, offering a safe space to neighborhood groups, and visiting members and non-members alike in the nearby nursing home. "All the decisions in the church depend on these three things. I can direct my preaching, teaching, and organizing to supporting the church as it does these."[6]

For other churches, the answer is not so clear.

An apparent lack of *purpose* may have many underlying causes. A church may have very good reasons for doing what it does, but these reasons may have been neglected or forgotten over time. Other churches find that their identity and mission need to evolve as the makeup of the church changes. A ministry that was important ten years ago may no longer be what the community needs or may no longer be what God is calling the church to do.

Educator and consultant Israel Galindo writes of the "lifespans" of churches. A new church often begins in excitement and develops a growing sense of its identity in its early years. Over time, it matures into a larger church with different members and ministries. Finally, a church may enter into a kind of old age, when the body seems more frail and restricted. Galindo observes that, along the way, churches

Ed the businessman says,
"A church I once belonged to decided it needed a new mission statement. They wanted to focus the church's activities, or something. It was good idea, except for the fact that after all the meetings and wordsmithing, the final statement was just so generic and bland. It never made us challenge ourselves. It never really got us going."

Ann the young pastor says,
"I guess I really made people uncomfortable, but in the long run, it was worth it. I kept asking, 'What is God calling us to do? What is God calling us to do? What is God calling us to do?' They got sick of me, but eventually we were able to say to ourselves and to our visitors exactly what God was calling us to do."

Dennis the bishop says,
"I love to see a church where they know they can make a difference. Whether they raise $50 or $5,000, they trust that their efforts, however modest, do glorify God and help others. And they connect worship and ministry profoundly. They see how the quality of worship, the preparation of the sermon, and the efforts of the choir to learn a tough piece all matter, because these contribute to a sense of sacred meaning in everything they do."

need to reinvigorate themselves with a fresh sense of identity and mission if they are to avoid the results of old age.[7] In the terms used in this book, churches need to *practice resurrection*. (See the Questions for Discussion at the end of this chapter for a more complete list of the stages in the lifespan of churches.)

The important question remains: Does a church have a clear sense of call from God, a clear reason why it should continue to meet and worship and serve? Pastor and author George B. Thompson Jr. stresses, "Keep in mind: the ultimate purpose for pastor and congregation getting along is to strengthen your church's gospel witness."[8]

Pastors and congregants who know why they are doing something tend to be more enthusiastic and better organized. And when people have a clear sense of God's *purpose*, they can indeed accomplish what God intends.

At my church, this Expectation is:

__**Not** Discussed   __**Not** Practiced

__**Not Widely** Agreed Upon   __**Not Widely** Practiced

__**Somewhat** Agreed Upon   __**Somewhat** Practiced

__**Widely** Agreed Upon   __**Widely** Practiced

__**Not** Applicable   __**Not** Applicable

6.3 Faithful pastors expect healthy congregations . . .
to believe that churches are called not to survive but to thrive.

"Churches that try to survive, don't."[9]

—a denominational executive

MANY OF THE PASTORS and laypeople I spoke with said their churches seemed to be in survival mode. As one lay leader confessed, "We speak about having enough money to 'keep the lights on,' but what we really mean is to 'keep the life-support machine on.'"[10] Indeed, some churches are just trying to hang on despite a sense of inevitable decline. Others just keep on doing what they've always done, convinced things are fine. In either case, such churches often lose their sense of *purpose*, either because they are afraid of the future or because they have achieved a level of comfort with the way things are. Survival seems like a fine goal.

But God does not call churches to survive. God calls churches to thrive—to thrive with the power of God at work in their midst. Thriving takes lots of forms—meaningful worship, steady ministry, deepening prayer lives, greater financial commitment, transformed lives. Machines and buildings do not "thrive," but living organisms do. Churches that flourish thus exhibit the characteristics of healthy living things; they develop and respond to changing circumstances by adapting. Not every church will grow in membership or be sustained in perpetuity, but every church can flourish, if only for a season. Small churches discover new ministries or revitalize old ones; whether they grow in membership or not, their members thrive as disciples.

Dennis the bishop says,
"Encouraging a church to close its doors is a harsh thing to say. No one likes closing a church. But no one likes seeing a church lose its purpose, either."

Rita the spiritual director says,
"Sometimes the most beautiful and purposeful times of a person's life are when she is dying. She accepts death but lives in victory. She has learned that what is important is not the continuation of breathing itself but the meaning that can come with each breath that is given to us."

Lisa the pharmacist says,
"Patients who have a reason for beating a disease seem to do a lot better than those who don't have something important they want to do."

Churches that try merely to survive, however, lack the vitality and *purpose* necessary for attracting new members or expanding congregational generosity. And churches that want to grow in number need to be clear about why. Visitors can sense when a church is seeking to attract new members only in order to keep the lights on. Merely hanging on just isn't very attractive or compelling. A visitor soon realizes her family is wanted primarily to help pay bills or serve on a committee, and she goes elsewhere. Hence, the denominational executive's saying quoted in the epigraph: "Churches that try to survive, don't."

By contrast, people recognize when a church has a sense of enthusiasm about its identity and mission. After all, there is pride in the fact that visitors are welcomed into something genuinely meaningful, something to be genuinely proud of.

Churches that "strive to thrive" exhibit a hopefulness that people want to be a part of.

At my church, this Expectation is:

__**Not** Discussed   __**Not** Practiced

__**Not Widely** Agreed Upon __**Not Widely** Practiced

__**Somewhat** Agreed Upon   __**Somewhat** Practiced

__**Widely** Agreed Upon   __**Widely** Practiced

__**Not** Applicable   __**Not** Applicable

6.4 Faithful pastors expect healthy congregations . . .
to trust that money follows mission.

"To sacrifice *literally means 'to make holy.' People are afraid to make sacrifices for church, and maybe that's because we don't see how our giving makes a difference."*[11]

—a United Methodist pastor

IT IS A SCENE REPEATED over and over again throughout the country. The leaders of a church gather and say to themselves, "We can't afford to . . ." In some very desperate cases, that is true. But in many, if not most, cases, congregants *could* give more. It is *not* true to say, "We can't afford to . . ." It *is* true to say, "We choose not to . . ." Congregations are not as trapped as they often think. Faithful pastors therefore experience the *eustress* required to encourage people to be the generous people they can become.

Healthy churches begin their budget process with discerning what God is calling the church to do in the coming year. Starting with the previous year's budget (which may look very similar to many previous budgets) presumes that God more or less wants everything to be the same, give or take a few percentage points. Over time, this pattern takes hold in the hearts of the congregation and sets profound limits on what the church is capable of discerning and imagining.

Starting the budget process with God's call can be frightening. What if God really is asking the people to try something new or to make more sacrifices? But if church members have a clear sense that increased giving will make a meaningful difference in the church, then the "sacrifice" indeed becomes making something holy. Healthy congregations trust that money follows mission. Discerning God's call for a church involves trusting God—and God's people!—to provide what is needed. How many churches restrict what God is capable of?

I remember a lay leader who always made it a point to object, in a loving way, to the church's annual balanced budget. He wanted to see an annual budget that projected a deficit. He wanted a budget, in other words, that would stretch the congregation's own expectations of itself and of God. He believed a church that sought to live within its own means was doing just that, living within its own means and not in God's bounty.

Bill the senior pastor says,

"I think budgets and the stewardship process are great for revealing how much we really care about the church. We tend to wring our hands about how we can't do this or that, or how we don't have enough money. The truth is that many of the members in some churches have all the money they need. Look at the houses people live in and the cars they drive. People will pay great sums of money for things that are important to them. If church is important enough, they'll support it."

Ed the businessman says,

"One of the best things my pastor ever did was to call me up and tell me I needed to give more money to the church. We both knew giving more was the right thing to do. He was respecting my call to serve our Lord."

Lisa the pharmacist says,

"If you are going to raise the cost, you've got to make it more valuable. People pay more for a fancy sports car because it means more to them. Churches are the same way—people pay for what they value. The question is, have the church leaders given the members a reason to value the church?"

When it clearly matters, people have no problem being incredibly generous.

At my church, this Expectation is:

__**Not** Discussed   __**Not** Practiced
__**Not Widely** Agreed Upon __**Not Widely** Practiced
__**Somewhat** Agreed Upon   __**Somewhat** Practiced
__**Widely** Agreed Upon   __**Widely** Practiced
__**Not** Applicable   __**Not** Applicable

6.5 Faithful pastors expect healthy congregations . . .
to take risks for the sake of the gospel.

"It is frightening to people that you have a call from God and are not yet fulfilling it."[12]

—a United Methodist pastor

IN MATTHEW 8:34–35, Jesus tells his disciples and the crowd that has gathered, "If any want to become my followers, let them deny themselves and take up their cross and follow me. For those who want to save their life will lose it, and those who lose their life for my sake, and for the sake of the gospel, will save it." Christians recognize that answering the call to follow Jesus involves making sacrifices (in terms of both time and money) and taking risks (e.g., welcoming people who look "different" into the church). Jesus' call to follow is unavoidably unsettling, even frightening.

Yet, for many Christians, the church represents a place of *safety*. At church, many Christians seek security amid the possibility of losing their jobs or the disturbing behavior of children. Christians find a peace and a calmness that allows them to relax. Christians find comfort in the friendly faces of people who love them for who they are. As their own bodies age, Christians feel relief in preserving an old church building. So how can a pastor preach on challenging passages such as Matthew 8:34–35 to a congregation that expects, even craves, *safety*?

Healthy congregations are not surprised when a pastor preaches on taking risks for the sake of the gospel. These churches recognize that while the church is indeed a place for *safety*, it is also a place for transformation, renewal, and, when necessary, death and *resurrection*. God loves us just as we are. But God loves us too much to leave us just as we are. God desires life abundant for God's people—and this life abundant does not come easily.

There are many risks a congregation may need to take. They may involve finances, worship, schedules, different ministries, or new programs. And they may involve the real possibility of failure, rejection, or embarrassment. Nevertheless, healthy pastors and faithful congregations hear Jesus when he says, "Do not be afraid."

Healthy churches are safe enough for people to take risks for the sake of the gospel.

Ann the young pastor says,
"One pastor I know tried repeatedly to encourage the lay leaders of her small church to invest in the church's future by starting a program and funding a new staff person. The lay leaders were cautious: What if things don't work out? The pastor started saying, 'If we have a problem with the budget, I'll go half time, and that will save the church about $20,000.' She did not want to go part time, but she was prepared to take a risk for her church."

Bill the senior pastor says,
"I think it is always helpful for churches to do a 'worst case scenario' when they are worried about something. What really happens if they can't afford to keep the utilities going? They can all go to a different church together and make a new place stronger with their experience, service, and money. This would be painful—but it is not as if one church's closing gets in the way of God's redemption of the world. When we look at it this way, we see how much of our own egos and our own personal needs we put into having our own churches."

At my church, this Expectation is:

___**Not** Discussed
___**Not Widely** Agreed Upon
___**Somewhat** Agreed Upon
___**Widely** Agreed Upon
___**Not** Applicable

___**Not** Practiced
___**Not Widely** Practiced
___**Somewhat** Practiced
___**Widely** Practiced
___**Not** Applicable

Rita the spiritual director says,
"Churches should be the place where we can take risks. I am uncomfortable letting a stranger into my house, but I am willing to work together with church members to open the church building for homeless people. I need a place that teaches me courage, the courage to take a chance when it is important. After all, prayer itself is a risk—when I pray 'Thy will be done,' I am putting my own will on the line."

6.6 Faithful pastors expect healthy congregations . . .
to recognize that all church members are called to lives of holy service.

"Good lay leaders help everyone say, 'I'm doing the thing I'm really called to do.'"[13]

—an Episcopal priest

PASTORS ARE *ORDAINED*, but God calls *all* people to serve.

Pastors seek to "equip the saints for the work of ministry" (Ephesians 4:12). The preaching, the teaching, the praying, the conversations over coffee, and the simple observations in the parking lot all work together to help everyone in the church become better disciples. One pastor spoke for many of those I interviewed when she said, "It's delightful to lead people when they are serious about growing as Christians."[14] Like a parent, teacher, or coach, pastors love to see people live up to their God-given potential.

But one of the dangers of having professional clergy, having people who are "set apart," is that churches will also set all the work apart for those people to do. So often, laypeople will say they don't know the Bible well enough, don't pray often enough, or don't know how to serve others in some form of ministry. Let the minister handle those—that's what we are paying him for. And pastors sometimes are all too happy to go along with this, since it makes them feel needed.

Healthy congregations realize that all baptized Christians are called to lives of prayer, Bible study, worship, service, and witness. This means that, in order to fulfill their own call, laypeople need to learn what might otherwise be the exclusive domain of the clergy. Pastors lead the people in prayer, but congregants need to learn how to pray, too. Pastors are trained to provide pastoral care, but all Christians are called to "bear one another's burdens" (Galatians 6:2). Vibrant congregations do not take it for granted that all members know how to worship and serve, and they seek to develop everyone's Christian "skill-set."

Churches that seek to grow spiritually in order to better fulfill God's *purpose* for them find that, in worship, Sunday school, and mission, they are indeed being "transformed by the renewing of [their] minds" (Romans 12:2).

Rita the spiritual director says,

"So often Christians feel so unworthy. Sometimes it is guilt or shame; sometimes they've absorbed countless messages of how they are not good enough. Listening to Christians breaks my heart because they have a hunger for God and a desire to care for others, yet they remain afraid and paralyzed. Here's where a good pastor and good friends at church can make a real difference."

Ed the businessman says,

"We had to get over a big divide in our church, the gap between those who focus on prayer and spirituality and those whose hearts are in community service. Our pastor introduced us to the idea of the 'inward-outward journey,' the idea that prayer shapes service and service shapes prayer. Each can become self-centered and exhausting without the other. When we began to think of these as going hand-in-hand, we looked at one another differently, and we saw that we all needed one another's gifts. Me? I like to pick up a hammer and go to work, but the prayer warriors in our church helped me to take the time and offer a little prayer before I start pounding away. It's hard to explain, but it has made a difference."

At my church, this Expectation is:

    __**Not** Discussed
    __**Not Widely** Agreed Upon
    __**Somewhat** Agreed Upon
    __**Widely** Agreed Upon
    __**Not** Applicable

    __**Not** Practiced
    __**Not Widely** Practiced
    __**Somewhat** Practiced
    __**Widely** Practiced
    __**Not** Applicable

Lisa the pharmacist says,
"What has really made a difference in our congregation is the fact that laypeople want to learn how to do things as Christians. We used to hear all the time about being peacemakers from the pulpit. But we never did anything until someone suggested we learn how to really be peacemakers, how to listen intentionally, how to practice conflict-resolution skills."

6.7 Faithful pastors expect healthy congregations . . .
to let the pastor be a pastor.

"My congregation expects me to do so many different things. I hardly have time to breathe, let alone pray or read the Bible."[15]

—a Presbyterian pastor

IN PERSONAL CONVERSATIONS and formal surveys, the most satisfied, energetic, and grateful pastors have overwhelmingly been pastors who feel they are using their gifts and their training effectively in their churches. This is no surprise—most people want their professional lives to be like this. People want to be valued for who they are and what they've learned to do. Joyful pastors are allowed to be the pastors God calls them to be.

Churches with a strong sense of *purpose* agree with Paul. God gives different gifts to different Christians (see Romans 12 and 1 Corinthians 12). And the church accepts the responsibility of placing the pastor and the members in positions to use their distinctive gifts. They organize the church in such a way that the pastor does what is truly important as a pastor.

In a healthy church, there is a sense that the pastor's work does make a difference. People say thank you for his leadership. The choir challenges itself to grow musically and spiritually in order to help the pastor lead worship. And members respond to God's work in their midst by actively serving others. Church members not only offer supportive comments about a sermon (or feel free to disagree respectfully!) but also ask the pastor to discuss it further with them later in the week (especially if they disagree!). And they feel comfortable working with the pastor to help him improve in needed areas. (See the appendix on conducting a Mutual Ministry Review.) There is, in short, a healthy sense of teamwork where the pastor is responsible for being the pastor and not the building supervisor or the outreach chair.

A church is blessed indeed when the pastor(s) and congregants share the profound delight that comes only from knowing that what they are doing is indeed part of what God is doing.

Lisa the pharmacist says,
"In the pharmacy, people trust me because of my training and experience, and because they know I have their best interests at heart. That's the way I feel about my pastor. In the pharmacy, people ask me about how a medicine works all the time. They want to get better, and they know that if they ask questions, I can maybe help them out. I try to look at my pastor that way, too. I worried that I was bugging her too much, but it soon became clear that she really liked talking about prayer and how to live a better Christian life. And just as I know not to judge people when they are taking medicine for conditions brought on by things they probably shouldn't have done, she is the same way when I talk about problems I brought on myself."

Ed the businessman says,
"I don't like the idea of needing pastoral care. But I know that if the pastor is too busy with things laypeople could do, she will not be able to provide the kind of loving, thoughtful pastoral care I will need in a crisis. Pastoral wisdom is not something a pastor turns on and off when needed. It takes regular cultivation and lots of hard work—and that means our church has to let the pastor be the pastor."

At my church, this Expectation is:

    __**Not** Discussed
    __**Not Widely** Agreed Upon
    __**Somewhat** Agreed Upon
    __**Widely** Agreed Upon
    __**Not** Applicable

    __**Not** Practiced
    __**Not Widely** Practiced
    __**Somewhat** Practiced
    __**Widely** Practiced
    __**Not** Applicable

Bill the senior pastor says,

"I've been in both kinds of churches—the ones where I could be a full-time pastor and the ones where I had to do lots of other things. I also learned the hard way that if I was going to be a pastor, sometimes I had to stop doing the other things."

Questions for You and Your Church

- Does your church have a mission statement? If so, can you provide specific examples of how it guides decision-making in the church?
- In his *The Hidden Lives of Congregations*, Israel Galindo describes the life-span of churches. He identifies a typical sequence that churches go through from founding and initial development (when there is great excitement, but perhaps a lack of direction) to adolescence and maturity (when the church usually takes on its core identity), to a time when a church's stability becomes solidified and rigid (when a church tends to lose its outward mission), to a period of almost bureaucratic hanging on (when an awareness of decline has begun to set in), and eventually to an end of the lifespan with the church's dissolution. How would you characterize your church's place in the lifespan? Galindo notes that this span is neither universal nor inevitable; a church can experience renewal that helps it regain its earlier sense of *purpose* or develop in new direction in response to God's leading. What might your church need to do?
- How do the people of your church live out the *eustress* of *safety* and risk-taking? Are you more concerned about *safety* or needing to do something different?
- Does your church's budgeting process suggest a church that is trying to survive or to thrive? Specifically, what signs do you see? How might your process be improved?
- How does your church support its members in their own calls to serve? How might your church better encourage people to serve God, their families, the church, or the local community?
- How do the congregation members and pastor of your church work together to let the pastor focus on his or her pastoral responsibilities? How might this process be strengthened?

7

Administration and Structure
ORGANIZING FOR EFFECTIVE MINISTRY

One of the greatest sources of stress for pastors is the fact that there is so much to do and so little time. Phone calls, emails, reports, people dropping by, lessons to prepare—and all of these tasks are just for one Sunday school class!

Often pastors lack clear guidance and support as to how they should allocate their time. When can the pastor leave the office in good conscience? That's not an easy question to answer, since the pastor knows her work is never done. And sometimes she wonders what Mr. Smith will say if something doesn't get done right and according to his timetable.

The central themes of this chapter are *accountability* and *mutual ministry*. This chapter draws on time management sections in other parts of the book, since a central challenge around *accountability* is the allocation of staff and volunteer time. Another concern is lay involvement in the life and mission of the congregation. Why do we accept the oft-used saying "20 percent of the people do 80 percent of the work" as "gospel"—especially when such behavior within congregations is far from the gospel? Perhaps we accept this 80–20 "rule" simply because it is what we have come to expect. Can we change our expectations?

Chapter 6 explored the importance of the *purpose* God has for a church community. This chapter presents a series of interwoven expectations that describe how a congregation and a pastor can together arrive at a better set of practices that will help them flourish as together they seek to fulfill that *purpose.*

Faithful pastors expect healthy congregations . . .
7.1 – to establish a clear, realistic job description for the pastor.
7.2 – to work collegially to determine priorities for pastoral ministry.
7.3 – to provide staffing and volunteers adequate for the church's life and mission.
7.4 – to engage in a Mutual Ministry Review for shared *accountability.*
7.5 – to establish a pastor-congregation relations team.
7.6 – to help provide continuing education for lay leaders.

7.1 Faithful pastors expect healthy congregations . . .
to establish a clear, realistic job description for the pastor.

"There are one hundred members in my church and one hundred job descriptions for the pastor."[1]

—a Baptist pastor

WHAT IS THE PASTOR supposed to do?

Some of the tasks are clear—preaching and leading worship are the most obvious. Pastoral care is also expected, as is administration.

But how much pastoral care and how much administration? The pastor will preach each Sunday (or work in rotation with other pastoral staff), but is the pastor responsible for visiting all the shut-ins? Does the pastor need to oversee the financial statements of the church on a monthly basis?

And how about plumbing? It's Friday afternoon, the pastor is the only one around, the sink in one of the bathrooms is clogged, and there is a funeral followed by a large reception planned for Saturday morning. Should the pastor continue working on the sermon, call a church member, or call a plumber? Church members may have other plans, and plumbers cost money. (Most plumbers get paid more per hour than most pastors.) Most pastors will say that plumbing ends up being in the job description. Indeed, one pastor told me that in addition to presenting a person being ordained with a Bible and stole, the church should also give the newly ordained pastor a screwdriver and a pipe wrench.

In addition to plumbing, financial oversight, and visitation, congregations sometimes assume—without stating it explicitly—that the pastor will have other responsibilities, like teaching Sunday school, leading mission trips, maintaining outreach programs, folding the bulletin, cleaning up the sanctuary, participating in ecumenical and interfaith organizations, organizing committees, and leading the weekday Bible study. Churches with more than one pastor often have job descriptions that clarify expectations as to who does what. Solo pastorates are far less likely to have such clarity.

Ed the businessman says,
"Church members need to be prepared to tell the pastor to stop fiddling with every problem that comes up in the church building. It might sound a little artificial in the normal flow of conversation, but something like 'The church does not set you apart with the laying on of hands in order to have you rewire the lamps in fellowship hall' would make the point nicely."

Dennis the bishop says,
"I love it when I see healthy functioning in a church. Clearly, identifying who is responsible for what through agreed-upon job descriptions for paid staff and volunteers does not solve all problems. But it a great step in the right direction. In some churches, I'm amazed at how much is assumed but left unsaid."

Bill the senior pastor says,
"Effective pastors don't do it all. They rejoice when lay members take ownership of the church, its common life, and its mission in the world. And they are willing to let some things in the church go undone until clarity about the limits of their own responsibility is agreed upon. Faithful pastors recognize that allowing short-term irritation in the congregation is sometimes necessary for healthy change and congregational development."

For their part, some pastors are all too eager to please or make a name for themselves, so they take on more responsibilities than they should. They observe few *boundaries* and encourage congregational underfunctioning by starting to overfunction (see Expectation 5.2).

So, what is the pastor actually supposed to do? Faithful pastors and healthy congregations recognize that, while there are many different tasks that *could* be done by the pastor, agreeing on what a pastor *should* be doing is fundamental if everyone is to thrive together.

Taking this first step of delineating the responsibilities of both pastor(s) and congregation is one of the most important things a community of faith can do to address the needs of effective ministry.

At my church, this Expectation is:

__**Not** Discussed   __**Not** Practiced
__**Not Widely** Agreed Upon   __**Not Widely** Practiced
__**Somewhat** Agreed Upon   __**Somewhat** Practiced
__**Widely** Agreed Upon   __**Widely** Practiced
__**Not** Applicable   __**Not** Applicable

7.2 Faithful pastors expect healthy congregations . . .

to work collegially to determine priorities for pastoral ministry.

"Pastor, please don't *come to the hospital to visit me. I'm fine, and preparing for the Sunday sermon is more important."*[2]

—a Presbyterian layperson

HEALTHY CONGREGATIONS and faithful pastors know the pastor should call someone to deal with a cracked windowpane instead of fixing it herself. But she still has a choice between working on the sermon or visiting someone in the hospital. Both are important things for a pastor to do. But which *should* she do? (The temptation may be to try and do both, perhaps at the expense of her family. See chapter 9.)

Pastors face this question on a daily basis. The problem gets even more complicated when there are disagreements or conflicts in the church. If the congregation and pastor do not agree on what tasks the pastor should prioritize, it becomes easy for disgruntled church members to say, "This church would be attracting new members if only the pastor would . . ."

Sometimes there is also another related phenomenon: people get so caught up in what seems urgent that they forget to do what is truly important. And without clear priorities, pastors are all too easily tempted to do what they *want* to do rather than what they *should* do. Most people prefer to work within their comfort zones; we all need help focusing our energies wisely and faithfully.

Working together to name what is truly important for the pastor to do is a great gift for the pastor and the congregation.

Most congregations live comfortably with the hope that everything can get done equally well. The process of prioritizing pastoral responsibilities can be challenging, but the entire community has to wrestle with the reality of limitations and choices. Congregations and pastors that take this important step take a great stride toward better self-understanding and increased clarity of *purpose*.

Rita the spiritual director says,
"If a church member complains that the pastor is not visiting people frequently enough, the supportive church member can reply, 'This may be true, but we've agreed that her priority should be preparing for the mission trip. Would you like to sign up for the visitation committee?'"

Dennis the bishop says,
"When a pastor does not have his priorities set, he ends up doing a lot of triage, always reacting to whatever immediate set of needs presents itself. People can do this for a while, but over time, they get tired and stressed, and they lose sight of the big picture. Sometimes they spend so much time doing one thing after another that they lose sight of what God is doing."

Ann the young pastor says,
"I try to reflect theologically on what is important for me to do in the congregation I serve. I am excited about the challenge of articulating for the congregation why one pastoral task should take priority over another. God has plans for us, great plans, but for us to respond to what God is doing, everyone needs to agree on what the pastor is supposed to be doing."

At my church, this Expectation is:

__**Not** Discussed

__**Not Widely** Agreed Upon

__**Somewhat** Agreed Upon

__**Widely** Agreed Upon

__**Not** Applicable

__**Not** Practiced

__**Not Widely** Practiced

__**Somewhat** Practiced

__**Widely** Practiced

__**Not** Applicable

7.3 Faithful pastors expect healthy congregations . . .
to provide staffing and volunteers adequate for the church's life and mission.

"There is an upper limit to the number of people a person can provide good care for. I'd put that at no more than twenty-five. A lot of listening is involved. And that takes time."[3]

—a spiritual director

EVEN AFTER THE CONGREGATION and pastor have established clear pastoral priorities, many needs remain. Who is answering the phones, photocopying the bulletins, leading the youth group, mowing the lawn, organizing the Habitat for Humanity workday, and making sure there are fresh flowers on Sunday morning? Should these tasks be done by paid staff or volunteers? And should the congregation take on additional staff or volunteers, people such as a parish nurse, a youth director, or a Christian educator?

Staffing—both paid and volunteer—is an opportunity for imagination and hope. All too easily, congregations think about staffing from a minimalist perspective: What do we need in order to keep going? Or, more bluntly, what do we need to (barely) get by? Churches rarely put it that way, but in effect they consider what is strictly *necessary* rather than what is truly *possible*. (See the discussion of surviving vs. thriving in 6.3.) How would staffing discussions be different if churches asked, "What do we need in order to thrive like never before?" Or "What is God challenging us to do?" Staffing boldly requires taking risks. But the gospel calls for taking risks. (Business people in the congregation might well recognize that thriving companies often call for increased staffing in anticipation of successful expansion.)

Inadequate staffing is a danger to the pastor-congregation *covenant*. Pastors have a primary responsibility for the functioning of the community, and they are often the ones who pick up the slack in weekly tasks. Folding the Sunday bulletin, answering the phones, and stuffing envelopes are necessary tasks, but they are a poor use of pastoral time.

In interviews for this book, spiritual directors, campus ministers, and choir directors—people in positions that nurture people intensively—reported that they could be effective with about 25–50 people at the most. Perhaps churches could step out in faith

Lisa the pharmacist says,

"Volunteering is important to me. I like doing things with friends at church. I'd like to see us grow and do some new things, and I know this is going to take time and money. But I figure if I do my part, this might encourage others not only to volunteer but also to have high hopes for what we can do as a church. I'm a very practical person, but it's the hoping and dreaming that keep me excited about church."

Rita the spiritual director says,

"There is a beautiful cycle. People become active in the life of a church and get some training, perhaps something that prepares people to care for others. Then, once they have some training and experience, they become more confident and comfortable. They see the value of what they are doing—not just for others but also for their own renewal. And so they want to do more, learn more, and grow into more. You'd think it would be exhausting, and sometimes it is. But with good guidance and support, this beautiful cycle is energizing."

and develop a plan for a bold ratio of paid and volunteer pastors, directors, mentors, and care-providers to congregants of 1:25. This would require dedicating additional resources to the life of God's church—but where better to devote our resources?

Healthy congregations develop a culture of cooperative endeavor. As the saying goes, "Many hands make for light work."

At my church, this Expectation is:

__**Not** Discussed
__**Not Widely** Agreed Upon
__**Somewhat** Agreed Upon
__**Widely** Agreed Upon
__**Not** Applicable

__**Not** Practiced
__**Not Widely** Practiced
__**Somewhat** Practiced
__**Widely** Practiced
__**Not** Applicable

Ed the businessman says,
"Businesses need the right number of people. Too many, and you pay too much salary; too few, and you can't meet the customer's needs. Churches are labor intensive because, in a way, everyone is a 'customer.' They all have needs—whether these are about worship or keeping the kitchen properly stocked with paper plates—and if you don't have enough folks doing enough things, people get unhappy."

7.4 Faithful pastors expect healthy congregations . . .
to engage in a Mutual Ministry Review for shared accountability.

"The individual approach [to ministry] has often resulted in clergy isolation and burnout, or blaming either the community by its clergy, or clergy by the community. . . . [This] approach also misses the abundant talent available to the community when ministry is seen as a common effort."[4]

—from the website of the Episcopal Diocese of Southern Virginia

WE ALL LIKE TO RECEIVE praise. But what about those times when things aren't working well? How do we handle those times when staff or volunteers don't show up or don't show up prepared?

Many employers have an annual review of employees. In theory, this provides an opportunity for improving the quality of work. In practice, it does not always work out that way, because no one wants to say anything negative or someone wants to use the process as a means of attack. Furthermore, reviewing performance once a year means things can go on for twelve months without being addressed. This gives time for unhelpful habits to form, and it increases the likelihood of resistance to useful change.

Churches that practice Mutual Ministry Reviews can address all of these dangers. When such a review is conducted in a spirit of mutual humility and eagerness for promoting the gospel as faithfully as possible, negative assessments can be received in a context of *safety* with openness and hope, not guilt and threat. Done well, these are times not of stress but of *eustress*.

The Mutual Ministry Review is a process that asks "How is Pastor Jane doing as pastor?" in the context of "How are we doing as a congregation?" The question of Pastor Jane's effectiveness remains, but it is set in the larger context of the congregation's responsibilities. The theme of *accountability* is understood both individually and communally. Is it possible that Pastor Jane's sermons would improve if she were not tracking down the volunteers who said they'd be there Sunday morning?

Rita the spiritual director says,
"People often don't like being reviewed at work or anywhere. We may not be secure enough in who we are to handle criticism, even constructive criticism. This is especially true at church, where many people are seeking refuge from their own fragility. People who give money and volunteer their time don't want to be 'assessed' for something they are giving freely. It just doesn't feel right. But if churches want to thrive, the leaders need the courage to be honest with one another about how things are going, what can be done better, and what people need in order to serve effectively."

Dennis the bishop says,
"Faithful pastors are prepared to listen to the concerns of the congregation. 'He just didn't listen!' is a frequent complaint from congregants when pastoral relationships end poorly. Mutual Ministry Reviews will not be successful if the pastor is not prepared to receive feedback with a spirit of learning and humility. On the other hand, a pastor who expresses gratitude for those helping him to become a better pastor is making it easier for others in the congregation to reflect on how they could be contributing more to the life of the church."

As appendix 1 further discusses, a Mutual Ministry Review allows congregations to celebrate their strengths while also identifying needs for improvement. (The review may suggest areas of church life in which there is a need to "practice *resurrection*.") This process also allows pastors and congregations to set—or reset—pastoral priorities. It may also yield insights about what *boundaries* need to be in place.

Accountability is often one of the hardest challenges for a congregation. But practiced faithfully, it prevents problems from festering and creates opportunities for healthier communities of faith. It helps everyone to "practice *resurrection*."

Ed the businessman says,
"A good business will always be checking itself, making sure people have what they need to do their jobs well. Part of making sure each person is doing his job is making sure that everyone is working together. It may be that one person's 'problem' has more to do with what other people are doing—or not doing."

At my church, this Expectation is:

__**Not** Discussed
__**Not Widely** Agreed Upon
__**Somewhat** Agreed Upon
__**Widely** Agreed Upon
__**Not** Applicable

__**Not** Practiced
__**Not Widely** Practiced
__**Somewhat** Practiced
__**Widely** Practiced
__**Not** Applicable

7.5 Faithful pastors expect healthy congregations . . .
to establish a pastor-congregation relations team.

"Don't Panic"[5]

—Douglas Adams

ALTHOUGH IT HAS A divine mandate, the church is also a human institution—and a Mutual Ministry Review sometimes brings up some issues that need to be addressed. This causes discomfort as everyone realizes that no one is perfect and that some changes need to be made. But this is good news. It is a sign of a faithful, healthy church community.

Still, working through problems and issues may not be easy.

Author and consultant Roy M. Oswald argues that a pastor-parish relations committee can help everyone.[6] He encourages every church to form a group of laypeople to meet regularly with the pastor in strict confidence. The group's focus is not so much on the tasks of the church as on the relationship between the pastor and the congregation. Whereas the Mutual Ministry Review would be conducted by church leaders in an official capacity, a pastor-congregation relations team would be a more informal group and would include laypeople not serving in official positions.

This team would look at how the pastor and members of the congregation are communicating—or not—in terms of the church's *purpose* and mutual respect for *ordination* and *covenant*. They would explore the effects of *eustress* on the community, asking whether *safety* is being sustained or increased. They are prepared to discuss questions of personal *maturity*. They are concerned about *accountability*, providing the pastor with a place to express concerns about the congregation (and vice versa!). Finally, they seek to promote and sustain healthy *boundaries*.

Unless there are dire needs, the discussions of this team remain confidential for the benefit of the pastor and those in the team. Outside the loop of formal reporting, this becomes a private arena for challenging conversations. For example, if church members were concerned that the pastor appears discouraged or frustrated, this would be a place where that concern might be discussed.

Lisa the pharmacist says,
"After all the conflict our congregation experienced, we decided we never again wanted to go through a time when people wouldn't speak to one another. We realized that our incoming pastor would need candid feedback. And we realized the congregation would need a way to communicate concerns informally. The pastor-congregation relations team was awkward at first, but it became natural. The flow of honest thoughts and feelings increased. Trust is hard to measure, but I believe it increased."

Ed the businessman says,
"I learned the hard way that a marriage covenant takes lots of work. A pastoral covenant takes lots of work too. You've got to keep working on the relationship, both addressing the problems and celebrating the good things. You can't let things fester, going to bed angry, and you've got to say 'I love you' or go on a date night regularly."

Bill the senior pastor says,
"There is a natural temptation for pastors to draw together a few laypeople they like—and who like them—and work only with these folks. But a wise pastor will avoid that kind of thing and seek advice and input from a wide range of people. Sometimes the person who most annoys you has the most to teach you."

While everyone likes being liked, the purpose of this team is not so much to make sure that the pastor is well liked. Rather, when these people meet, their focus is on whether the relationship is healthy. This team is not "for" or "against" the pastor or anyone in the church; it is "for" the healthy relationship between pastor and congregation. The pastor and congregants should be speaking and listening, expressing disagreements in respectful ways, and demonstrating a common desire to thrive together.

A pastor-congregation relations team is not so much a place for "venting" (though that may need to happen sometimes), but rather a good place for addressing dynamics within the community before they get to the need-to-vent stage.

At my church, this Expectation is:

__**Not** Discussed   __**Not** Practiced
__**Not Widely** Agreed Upon   __**Not Widely** Practiced
__**Somewhat** Agreed Upon   __**Somewhat** Practiced
__**Widely** Agreed Upon   __**Widely** Practiced
__**Not** Applicable   __**Not** Applicable

7.6 Faithful pastors expect healthy congregations . . .
to help provide continuing education for lay leaders.

"We expect so much from our lay leaders. But do we develop and sustain them?"[7]

—a Disciples of Christ pastor

A MUTUAL MINISTRY REVIEW process and a pastor-congregation relations team require laity who are well prepared to serve the church. Most churches have annual officer trainings that provide important information about the organizational, theological, and liturgical life of the church. But what happens after the training concludes? All too often, that is where things stop. Lay leaders can get by—but will they thrive?

Churches and pastors benefit greatly when lay leaders sustain their training. People who feel equipped are more likely to serve and to serve more confidently. People who read about other churches are able to see new possibilities for their own—or to appreciate their own church's unique gifts. And lay leaders who study excellent books on how congregations can thrive together with their pastors in a covenantal relationship are well prepared to do just that.

Faithful pastors encourage this process of continuing education for the laity. They are called "to equip the saints for the work of ministry" (Ephesians 4:12), and this includes being willing to let others become "experts" in the church. Healthy congregations have lay leaders who welcome this opportunity and are willing to commit the time needed for continuing education.

There are many resources available to congregations and lay leaders—books, periodicals, websites, to name just a few. Denominations often provide educational events that can be incredibly helpful for those who attend. Training programs like Stephen Ministry or programs offered through organizations such as the Center for Congregational Health, the Alban Institute, the initiative on leadership education at Duke Divinity School, and the Center for Congregations provide many different ways a congregation can nurture its leaders. Being a serious, committed,

Lisa the pharmacist says,
"I asked my pastor for resources on environmental stewardship. I didn't want to be a bother, but I was genuinely curious. He was excited that someone wanted to know more, and while he didn't know much himself, he knew where to go to find more information. He takes his role as a teacher very seriously, and I think my 'bothersome' request was actually a refreshing gift."

Ed the businessman says,
"We decided to put a line item in our budget for our lay leaders' continuing education needs. The reasoning was that for a few hundred dollars, the whole church would benefit by having better prepared church officers. Each person did something different—bought books or subscribed to magazines or attended a conference. I think they also appreciated being supported by the congregation."

Ann the young pastor says,
"There is so much out there! I didn't want to graduate from seminary because I wanted to learn more about all kinds of things—youth work, mission trips, fundraising, strategic planning, leading small groups, strategies for encouraging volunteers. What if our congregation had a church-leadership book club and covenanted together to read something once a month? I can only imagine how much we'd grow in confidence and abilities."

engaged Christian takes time and effort. Churches can make it easier by supporting lay education.

Prioritizing the time and resources needed for the ongoing training of lay leaders benefits the entire congregation. As these women and men grow as disciples and develop their gifts, they serve with greater energy and effectiveness.

At my church, this Expectation is:

__**Not** Discussed   __**Not** Practiced

__**Not Widely** Agreed Upon   __**Not Widely** Practiced

__**Somewhat** Agreed Upon   __**Somewhat** Practiced

__**Widely** Agreed Upon   __**Widely** Practiced

__**Not** Applicable   __**Not** Applicable

Questions for You and Your Church

- How often do the pastor and lay leaders of your church discuss the pastor's job description or pastoral priorities? How often are these things discussed with the congregation? How might having such conversations be helpful?
- Does your congregation exhibit the 80–20 phenomenon—20 percent of the people do 80 percent of the work? If so, how might you change that?
- What would the church do if a seminary student said that she wanted to volunteer at the church for eight hours a week as part of her training? Where would those "extra hours" make the most difference?
- Are reviews of the pastor, staff, and volunteers done in your church? If so, are these reviews useful? Why or why not? If your church does not have a Mutual Ministry Review process, can you see some advantages to developing one? What obstacles might you see to implementing one?
- Does your church have a pastor-congregation relations team? If so, how is it working? If not, would your church benefit from one?
- How might the lay leaders of your congregation benefit from opportunities for continuing education? What would they enjoy learning more about? Can your church recognize their dedication by supporting their ongoing study in some way?

8

Supporting the Pastor
A COVENANTAL APPROACH

Consider the following: A lay leader at an Episcopal church was known for saying over and over again, "You've got to take care of your clergy." On his deathbed, a person at a Presbyterian church remembered his pastor of many years ago, sighed, and said, "We did him wrong."A United Methodist pastor responded to the question of how he could be better supported by his congregation by saying, "If they acknowledged me as a human being."[1]

The way a congregation supports its pastor is important. A healthy congregation takes its *covenant* with its pastor seriously and exhibits pride in caring for the pastor. They think of her welfare when making decisions. Even when there are disagreements, they work with their pastor in a spirit of trust and hope. In turn, their pastors offer years of sustained service.

But in other congregations, church members neglect to recognize that the pastor is a person just like they are. Consciously or unconsciously, they view the pastor more like a contractual employee. They have little interest in developing healthy *boundaries*. They will hold him accountable, but they are not so interested in their own *accountability*.

The good news is that most churches seek to be good, healthy places for their pastors. This chapter and the next (on supporting the pastor's family) may help congregations develop better habits of taking care of their clergy.

Faithful pastors expect healthy congregations . . .
8.1 – to help them see that their *mutual ministry* is making a difference.
8.2 – to pray for the pastor.
8.3 – to provide honest feedback, including both appreciation and constructive criticism.
8.4 – to hold the pastor accountable and practice forgiveness.
8.5 – to provide appropriate financial support.
8.6 – to provide for time off and a regular sabbatical.
8.7 – to value the pastor's time dedicated to prayer and study as an integral part of his service to the church.
8.8 – to give pastors freedom to be themselves and to respect each pastor's unique sense of call.

8.1 Faithful pastors expect healthy congregations . . .
to help them see that their mutual ministry is making a difference.

"My greatest joy in ministry? Watching people step outside their comfort zones and do something new for Christ."[2]

—a United Methodist pastor

LIKE EVERYONE ELSE, pastors want to know that they are making a difference.

When I asked pastors what congregations could do to help them the most, they said they most wanted to see their congregations striving to be faithful to God and God's call for them. The most important thing for pastors is seeing that all the energy they put in and all the sacrifices they make—lower salary, inconvenient work hours, and stress—are somehow benefiting God's kingdom.

In healthy churches, pastors arrive home at the end of the day and can recall the goodness of the day as they brush their teeth. They have seen laity involved in the life and work of the church, and have seen, for example, a shy person come to enjoy serving as the liturgist.

In unhealthy situations, pastors wonder if it is all worth it. They grumble (to themselves or to their spouses) about money, isolation, or troublesome church members. Nothing done out of love is done in vain, but pastoral service done out of grumbling comes with no such guarantee.

Pastoring is hard to evaluate and almost impossible to quantify. (Changes in membership or giving are not always reliable indicators of a pastor's effectiveness.) And there are numerous reasons why pastors may have a hard time seeing the significance of their efforts. They may be under too much stress or too exhausted to see the good things around them. They may have unrealistic or inappropriate expectations of the congregation, so they fail to see healthy progress. They may be overfunctioning, and the congregation may have started underfunctioning (see Expectation 5.2). And ultimately, they simply may not, in fact, be serving effectively.

The Mutual Ministry Review (see appendix 1) provides a formal way for congregation members to reflect together with the pastor on precisely this question of how her leadership is making a difference. But

Rita the spiritual director says,

"A member of a church can offer a tremendous blessing by asking, 'What is it about my pastor that helps me the most?' If a person can search her heart, name this, and then share that with her pastor, this act of deepest honesty will be a great gift. The pastors I know are struggling. Like Ezekiel, they have a fire in their bones for God and their churches. Passion means literally 'to suffer' and for many pastors, their passion for their people is a kind of suffering. They very much need to hear that their efforts are helping others."

Lisa the pharmacist says,

"A number of us made it a monthly habit of naming thanksgivings and blessings in the life of the congregation. We'd meet with the pastor before worship and talk about how a ministry was going or how someone seemed to be more engaged in the life of the church. This helped us all recognize that God was at work in our midst. This was especially helpful when we had to deal with a tight budget."

informal words of thanksgiving and encouragement from church members help provide the regular renewal needed to sustain a faithful pastor.

We tend to think of pastors as strong and faithful. Most are—but that does not mean they don't need help seeing the significance of what they do.

At my church, this Expectation is:

    __**Not** Discussed
    __**Not Widely** Agreed Upon
    __**Somewhat** Agreed Upon
    __**Widely** Agreed Upon
    __**Not** Applicable

    __**Not** Practiced
    __**Not Widely** Practiced
    __**Somewhat** Practiced
    __**Widely** Practiced
    __**Not** Applicable

Bill the senior pastor says,
"A pastor who is having a hard time seeing God at work in his congregation may benefit from looking at the congregation in a different way. Instead of lamenting how the members need to be more Christ-like, he might ask how the members already are Christ-like. Just because they are not disciples in the ways the pastor wants does not mean that God is not at work in their midst."

8.2 Faithful pastors expect healthy congregations . . .
to pray for the pastor.

"We expect our pastor to be so close to God and yet there is such a huge emotional burden, so much that he has to deal with, our emergencies, crises, our stuff. Shouldn't we be lifting him up in prayer?"[3]

—a Presbyterian lay leader

IN MY EXPERIENCE one of the most beautiful aspects of being a pastor is hearing from congregants that they are praying for you. The love and hope that congregants express can be palpable. Pastors are drawn into the mystery of the fact that so many people are thinking of them as they say their prayers at night. This is humbling and deeply moving. And it makes a difference.

For ministers, knowing their congregations are praying for them helps them remain properly focused. Ministry is God's work, not theirs. And part of God's response to prayer is helping everyone see how we are drawn closer to one another as we draw closer to God in prayer. Pastors and church members who pray regularly for one another are able to face the tough times of inevitable disagreement and conflict because there is already a foundation of love and mutual support.

This book is in large part about the challenges facing pastors and the ways congregations can help. Pastors need prayer for many things in the course of just one week: faithfulness in preaching; courage to stand up for what God wants; discernment about whether to change family plans because of an emergency phone call; concerns about the congregation's financial future. Healthy congregations do God's work by helping their pastors.

In his *The Contemplative Pastor,* pastor and author Eugene Peterson says, "My primary educational task as a pastor was to teach people to pray."[4] Pastors like to pray—but they also like it when others pray for them. After all, it is a sign that their ministry is making a difference.

Ann the young pastor says,
"I have a friend in the congregation who makes a difference for me. When she knows I am heading toward a difficult visit or wrestling with a problem, she will insist on praying for me at the end of our conversation. And she prays right then and there, in person or over the phone. Has anyone ever prayed that way for you, lifting your name up to God for help? If so, you can sense how important this is."

Dennis the bishop says,
"Something really sticks in my mind— during a healing and wholeness service in a particular church, a dozen or so people came forward from the congregation and kneeled to receive prayer, the laying on of hands, and anointing with oil. During this time, the prayerful attention of everyone in the church was focused on the kneeling person. When the pastor eventually turned from facing the congregation and leading the prayers to facing in the same direction as the congregation and kneeling down to be prayed over, he started crying. He was someone for whom worshipping was largely about focusing on others. Here, in this moment, he let go of his responsibilities, received prayers, and knew he was loved."

At my church, this Expectation is:

___**Not** Discussed
___**Not Widely** Agreed Upon
___**Somewhat** Agreed Upon
___**Widely** Agreed Upon
___**Not** Applicable

___**Not** Practiced
___**Not Widely** Practiced
___**Somewhat** Practiced
___**Widely** Practiced
___**Not** Applicable

Ed the businessman says,
"In the Roman Catholic church, prayers are offered in worship for the clergy, bishop, and pope. In Protestant churches, pastors generally don't want to lead public prayers for themselves. What would happen if laypeople said they would like time in the Sunday service to pray for the pastor and the leadership in the church, a time to express gratitude and ask for the Spirit's ongoing aid?"

8.3 Faithful pastors expect healthy congregations . . .
to provide honest feedback, including both appreciation and constructive criticism.

"It's hard to assess your ministry. You are not sure if you have done a good job. . . . There is no easy yes or no on the task and whether it was done right."[5]

—a United Methodist pastor

A PASTOR PREACHED for the first time at a congregation. After the service, as he was greeting congregants at the door, an elderly member of the church took his hands, looked deeply into his eyes, and said, "That was the most meaningful sermon I ever heard." He looked down, both thrilled and humbled, and noticed she was wearing one brown shoe and one blue shoe. This did not invalidate the truthfulness of her statement, but it did suggest to him that maybe her feedback should be understood differently.

We all like praise when it is honest, and we all need constructive criticism when it is faithful. Sometimes the ritual handshake at the church door does convey genuine appreciation to a pastor. But the polite "I enjoyed your message" can be so polite that it is hard to know what it really means. Like all who takes their craft seriously, a faithful pastor actually might prefer criticism that helps her to serve more effectively. I've known a congregant who regularly tells the pastor what the sermon should have been about. The pastor appreciates this because it is a sign of meaningful, respectful relationship in which the Word of God is taken seriously.

Healthy congregations speak the truth in love, naming both strengths and areas for improvement in a pastor's service. The Mutual Ministry Review process also identifies ways the congregation can help; the pastor is not left alone on an island.

Some unhealthy congregations pile on the criticism, making the pastor feel as if nothing is ever good enough. Other unhealthy congregations are hesitant to say anything negative; they deprive the minister of an opportunity for growth—and thereby deprive themselves of the opportunity for becoming a better church.

Healthy congregations nurture great pastors by being honest about what's going well, what needs

Ann the young pastor says,

"There are some things my congregation does that I really appreciate. If someone did not understand something in the sermon or the service, that person will ask me about it. Sometimes I realize I need to find a different way to express my ideas. Or if there is something someone likes, he or she will say something specific—not just 'good sermon' but 'The story about the nurse helped me see what you were getting at.' And I don't mind at all if they ask me to slow down when I speak. That means that they want to listen!"

Dennis the bishop says,

"Congregations should expect faithful pastoral leadership, and they have a responsibility for nurturing their pastor or pastors. All too often congregations expect that a pastor who is called to the church will show up all ready to do a great job. Pastors are like everyone else: they've got strengths and weaknesses in what they do. And vibrant congregations appreciate the strengths and figure out ways to address the weaknesses. Good pastors will be eager for this kind of cooperative work."

improvement, and how they can work together to make things better.

At my church, this Expectation is:

___**Not** Discussed
___**Not Widely** Agreed Upon
___**Somewhat** Agreed Upon
___**Widely** Agreed Upon
___**Not** Applicable

___**Not** Practiced
___**Not Widely** Practiced
___**Somewhat** Practiced
___**Widely** Practiced
___**Not** Applicable

Ed the businessman says,
"The best professionals—be they football players, teachers, or pastors—are always asking, 'How can I improve?' They recognize they are far from perfect and that they need the help of others. And when people try to help them, the best professionals receive the advice or criticism not with offended pride but with deep gratitude."

8.4 Faithful pastors expect healthy congregations . . .
to hold the pastor accountable and practice forgiveness.

"If I've done something wrong, I want to know."[6]

—a Baptist pastor

HEALTHY FEEDBACK and good practices of providing constructive criticism may not solve every problem. What happens when the pastor persists in behavior or practices that hinder or even harm the congregation?

Chapter 1 identified *covenant, resurrection, safety, maturity,* and *accountability* as foundational principles for a vibrant church. All of these are involved when it comes to holding the pastor accountable and practicing forgiveness.

Covenant reminds us that the pastor's welfare is a concern of the church. *Resurrection* lifts up the fact that the pastor may need to let some of her habits die so better ones may live. *Safety* is required for difficult conversations, especially if one party is going to have a hard time hearing what is said. *Maturity* allows everyone to speak honestly without making personal attacks. And *accountability* itself is a sign of a healthy relationship; it is not easy for one person to talk to another and ask him to reflect on the adequacy of what he is doing.

When *accountability* is practiced with all these in mind, the guilt and shame that otherwise would be present for the pastor can give way to the joy of forgiveness that the congregation also expresses. And when we know we are indeed forgiven despite our mistakes, our trust and love increase. Indeed, our desire to become more faithful grows, too. And so we come to serve in gratitude and hope, not fear.

No one likes to be held accountable. But there is wisdom behind Hebrews 12:6: "The Lord disciplines [holds accountable] those whom he loves."

Dennis the bishop says,
"The congregation needs to be prepared to help a pastor who has demonstrated abiding problems with some pastoral functions. Funding may be needed to provide extra training for the pastor or to hire a consultant or advisor. There is nothing wrong or shameful about this. It is part of the way God is at work in the congregation, bringing everyone to a better place. Matthew 18 reveals that God expects us to be prepared to hold others accountable: 'If another member of the church [including the pastor!] sins against you, go and point out the fault when the two of you are alone. If the member listens to you, you have regained that one' (Matt. 18:15). I like to advise congregations that they can 'regain' their pastors."

Bill the senior pastor says,
"I remember once when I'd made some decisions without consulting people. I really angered some folks. I'm glad two congregants came and talked with me. It was awkward and embarrassing, and I really had to work hard to listen. It gave me a chance to apologize—and a chance to talk with them about why I did what I did. The church could have gone sour if those two didn't come speak with me. They demonstrated a trust in God that I respected, and they demonstrated a trust in me that made me want to do better next time."

At my church, this Expectation is:

__**Not** Discussed
__**Not Widely** Agreed Upon
__**Somewhat** Agreed Upon
__**Widely** Agreed Upon
__**Not** Applicable

__**Not** Practiced
__**Not Widely** Practiced
__**Somewhat** Practiced
__**Widely** Practiced
__**Not** Applicable

Ed the businessman says,
"It is not easy to suggest to the pastor that something he is doing is troublesome to you. If you have a serious problem, the first thing to do is to trust God will be at work in your conversation if you approach the problem in love and hope. The second thing to do is to realize that a faithful pastor will appreciate your honesty in coming directly to him."

8.5 Faithful pastors expect healthy congregations . . .
to provide appropriate financial support.

"Pastors struggle with money and paying the bills just like everyone else."[7]

—a United Methodist pastor

PEOPLE DO NOT BECOME pastors in order to get rich. Indeed, many a second-career pastor has to accept a cut in pay as part of his or her response to God's call. Still, as the Old Testament example of the Levites and Paul's directions in Galatians 6:6 make clear, a local church has a covenantal responsibility to provide appropriate financial support (see also 1 Corinthians 9:14 and 3 John 1:8).

But what is "appropriate financial support"? This is different from asking, "What can a church afford?" or "How much can I get as the pastor?" The former is a question of *covenant*, in that it is attentive to the well-being of the pastor as well as of the church. The latter questions are contractual, because they are concerned primarily, perhaps exclusively, with one party's self-interested point of view.

A pastor making $50,000 per year in total compensation (a median salary for some denominations) and working a typical sixty-hour week with six weeks off for vacation and study leave would be making a little over $18/hour, exclusive of benefits. Is this appropriate for someone in the middle of her career?

The skill set required of effective pastors—administrative leadership, public speaking, listening skills, and self-discipline (to name but a few)—are skills that are also valued in other professions, professions that often pay two or three times what pastors typically receive. Should pastors receive the median salary (and benefits) of professionals in the congregation? Should they be paid the same as lawyers, doctors, or social workers in the area? Many pastors have children they want to send to college and would like to own a home, just like anyone else. Are churches helping their pastors remain pastors?

Pastors know the budget as well as anyone in the church. They are well aware that any money their churches might give to them could also be used to strengthen the youth group, hire a first-rate musician

Rita the spiritual director says,

"Pastoral ministry is based on the model of Jesus, the Good Shepherd. This Shepherd, according to John 10, is not a hired hand who runs away at the first sign of danger but someone willing to lay down his life for the sheep. Churches must never view their pastor as someone they hire—otherwise they may hire someone who does not commit himself fully to serving them."

Ed the businessman says,

"People say, 'You get what you pay for.' I think churches often get more from their pastors than what they pay for. What troubles me is the fact that we value what we pay for. If you pay more for a car, you value it more. If you get something on the cheap, you value it less. It's human nature—and I am worried that this applies to how much churches value their pastors, too."

Dennis the bishop says,

"Churches often don't think about cost-of-living increases for their pastors. When the cost of food and gas goes up, the value of the amount of money the church gives to the pastor goes down. If churches don't, at the very least, build in cost-of-living increases for their pastors and other staff, they are saying, in effect, 'We are paying you less this year.'"

for Easter, or go to one of the church's ministries. Pastors care deeply about their churches, and may be more concerned about their churches than themselves (and perhaps even their own families). Lay leaders may need to advocate for the pastor at budget time.

Captain Chesley Sullenberger, the pilot who in January 2009 successfully landed a passenger plane in the Hudson River after it lost its engine power, now advocates for the future of his own profession. Underpaying pilots, he believes, will ultimately lead otherwise-qualified people away from the profession.[8] How many resist the call to ministry—or never even think about it as a possibility—because of enduring patterns of inadequate compensation?

Healthy churches recognize the importance of providing for their pastors. These congregations feel more generous, and they have higher expectations of their leaders.[9]

At my church, this Expectation is:

__**Not** Discussed   __**Not** Practiced
__**Not Widely** Agreed Upon   __**Not Widely** Practiced
__**Somewhat** Agreed Upon   __**Somewhat** Practiced
__**Widely** Agreed Upon   __**Widely** Practiced
__**Not** Applicable   __**Not** Applicable

8.6 Faithful pastors expect healthy congregations . . .
to provide for time off and a regular sabbatical.

"We had a pastor who did not take time off for himself. He ended up in the hospital. Twice."[10]

—a Presbyterian lay leader

THE COVENANTAL RELATIONSHIP between pastor and congregation leads healthy congregations to provide for times of rest and refreshment for their pastors, both on a regular basis and after years of service. Pastors consistently report long hours and high stress. As one pastor said, "My greatest frustration is my inability to get away."[11]

While everyone can understand the benefits of having days off during the week or taking vacations, the importance of a pastoral sabbatical is less clear. Modeled on the pattern of Sabbath rest in Scripture, sabbaticals allow pastors to step back from years of intense service in order to rest, reflect, and renew. Pastors often report that they need periods of sustained reading, prayer, and learning. They have ideas, notions, and hopes, but the regular guidance of a church precludes their going into things very deeply. Expectation 5.4 stated that healthy congregations expect faithful pastors to take a sabbatical; this section recognizes the other part of the *covenant*—that faithful pastors expect healthy congregations to make this possible.

A healthy church setting has three things that make this possible: (1) strong lay leadership that can function independently of the pastor, (2) the financial resources to provide for pastoral leadership during the sabbatical time, and (3) a pastor who can be away from the church (see Expectation 10.5 on avoiding fusion and codependence).

Many denominations now have official policies (or unofficial recommendations) regarding paid sabbaticals. These suggest appropriate lengths (usually two months or so after six years of service) as well as strategies for what pastors and churches should (and should not) be doing during the season of rest and what is expected of the pastor upon return to the church.

Denominational leaders recognize the importance of sabbaticals because they work with burnt-out pastors and congregations that have suffered because of

Rita the spiritual director says,
"I was so saddened by how one pastor described his congregation. He said members made jokes about his taking time off or going on vacation as if he weren't already working hard enough. How could congregants do that? They wouldn't tolerate those kinds of things in their own employment."

Ed the businessman says,
"Set aside the money from the beginning. That was our lesson when we wanted our pastor to have a sabbatical. Because we didn't have any money set aside over the years, we suddenly had to come up with the cash. It was a stretch, but we did it because keeping our pastor refreshed and happy is in everyone's interest."

Bill the senior pastor says,
"Pastors who would like a sabbatical might think that coming into church looking exhausted and stressed would be helpful. More helpful would be a consistent strategy of equipping the laity to function in their absence. If they do that, they can also get a day off every now and then."

pastoral exhaustion. No one wants a weary pastor (just as no one wants a weary doctor or lawyer). Everyone benefits from refreshment. A renewed pastor is better able to lead a congregation toward health and vibrancy.

Appreciating the importance of a sabbatical comes from recognizing the benefits both the congregation and the pastor receive.

At my church, this Expectation is:

__Not Discussed **__Not** Practiced
__Not Widely Agreed Upon **__Not Widely** Practiced
__Somewhat Agreed Upon **__Somewhat** Practiced
__Widely Agreed Upon **__Widely** Practiced
__Not Applicable **__Not** Applicable

8.7 Faithful pastors expect healthy congregations . . .
to value the pastor's time dedicated to prayer and study as an integral part of his service to the church.

"If we have no life in Christ, we have no ministry."[12]

—Andrew Purves

EXPECTATION 4.4 STRESSED that healthy congregations expect their pastors to be learning and growing constantly. Expectation 8.7—that faithful pastors expect their congregations to support them in this growth—is a kind of covenantal twin to 4.4.

Most pastors estimate that it takes between ten and fifteen hours to plan a worship service and prepare a sermon. People notice when a sermon is poorly prepared or the service shows signs of inattentiveness. And people appreciate the difference when the pastor is able to take the time to review the sermon several times and eliminate rambling and unnecessary points.

Not only does worship benefit from regular hours of study and prayer, but pastoral care also requires a pastor who lives and breathes the Word. For a pastor to help a person understand her situation in theological terms, the pastor needs to be deeply engaged with the Bible, theology, ethics, and other disciplines. If a pastor would be a non-anxious presence in a hospital room, she needs to be listening to and speaking with God regularly in prayer.

Pastors know that reading biblical commentaries or setting aside time for prayer means they will have less time available to visit congregants or address administrative needs. But pastors also know that proficiency with Scripture and prayer are the foundations of ministry. Faithful pastors expect healthy congregations to respect the importance of study and prayer—even if it means that less "work" gets done.

Healthy churches make sure the pastor has plenty of time for study and prayer by making sure that the pastor is not having to do it all herself. Healthy churches realize that everyone benefits if someone other than the pastor is taking care of the property or the budget.

Rita the spiritual director says,
"The greatest gift a pastor has to offer is her life with God. Preaching, worship, visiting, setting priorities, leading a mission trip—all these flow from a vibrant life with God. And this life is like a splendid flower—it sustains its beauty only with cultivation. Some pastors grow dry spiritually and end up having very little to offer. Is it any wonder their churches are not developing?"

Ann the young pastor says,
"The only analogy I can think of for the importance of my devotional time—my time for prayer and Bible study—is music. There are musicians who just play the notes on the score, and there are musicians who bring a living, vibrant, human quality to the music. Great musicians live the music and bring this life to the stage hours after hours of practice, exploring, and even fooling around with their instruments. They have a mastery and a freedom that is far beyond the technical achievement of getting the notes right. I want to be a pastor that does more than get the notes right."

At my church, this Expectation is:

  __**Not** Discussed
  __**Not Widely** Agreed Upon
  __**Somewhat** Agreed Upon
  __**Widely** Agreed Upon
  __**Not** Applicable

  __**Not** Practiced
  __**Not Widely** Practiced
  __**Somewhat** Practiced
  __**Widely** Practiced
  __**Not** Applicable

Ed the businessman says,
"The congregation can support the pastor's time for prayer and study by doing two things: one, establish these as priorities as part of an annual or semi-annual review, and two, make it clear to any who complain that the church expects a prayerful, learned pastor and that this takes time. Lay leaders who are prepared to advocate for the mutually agreed upon priorities of the pastor can be one of a church's greatest assets."

8.8 Faithful pastors expect healthy congregations . . .
to give pastors freedom to be themselves and to respect each pastor's unique sense of call.

"My greatest frustration in ministry is not knowing how much of myself to reveal."[13]

—a United Methodist pastor

IN HEALTHY RELATIONSHIPS, people enjoy one another's quirks and foibles—and may even tease each other gently about them. An individual's unusual food preferences, passion for a particular sports team, or ability to quote in great detail from *Star Wars* movies (and even the novels) is not a cause for alarm, but rather simply a part of what make that person special, even lovable. By contrast, in unhealthy relationships, these things become targets of opportunity: "If he didn't waste so much time with Luke Skywalker, he'd be a much better . . ."

One sign of a healthy church is when a pastor's quirks and eccentricities are welcomed. I happen to love watching professional football (and reading about it on various websites). One of the loveliest gifts I've ever received was a football signed by members of the church. They were showing their affection for me not just as a pastor but also as a particular person. In that church, I was free to be myself—warts (or fumbles) and all.

Not every church gives its pastor that freedom. Sometimes, in subtle or not so subtle ways, churches tell their pastors that they want them to conduct themselves according to certain standards. These requirements may involve not just hobbies or even drinking a glass of wine but also leadership styles and even the content of sermons. And these may have more to do with who the previous pastor was than with who the current pastor actually is.

A consensus-builder may be told to be a more forceful leader. Someone committed to cultivating personal piety may be told to preach more on contemporary social issues. A congregation may show absolutely no interest whatsoever in a pastor's passion for a local food bank. Certainly, pastors need to attend to the needs of the congregation; pastoral ministry should never be all about the pastor. But healthy churches appreciate the unique qualities of their pastors and honor their particular gifts and interests.

Dennis the bishop says,
"When a congregation and a pastor are in a covenantal relationship, each side remembers that the well-being of the other is of great importance. A congregation does well to recognize that the distinctive personality and ministry focus of its pastor are inherent parts of the relationship. Letting the pastor be her own person leads to a more energetic pastor. The Bible gives us many different models for spiritual leadership—Paul, Peter, the Beloved Disciple, not to mention the various prophets. There's no one way to be a pastor, so it is good when the pastor can be herself."

Rita the spiritual director says,
"Ministry must be genuine, honest, from the heart. Pastors need to be themselves, not someone the congregation wants them to be or something they think they should be. As with pastors, so, too, are people in the congregation burdened by trying to be someone they are not. Sometimes the greatest act of ministry is for a pastor to be himself. Nurturing a great pastor means nurturing the pastor's ability to be comfortable with who he is."

Pastors are called to serve a church—and they are called to that place because of who they are. There is an astounding normalcy to many of the best pastors. They are real people with real quirks. They help others realize that being a Christian does not mean being extraordinary or strange.

At my church, this Expectation is:

___**Not** Discussed
___**Not Widely** Agreed Upon
___**Somewhat** Agreed Upon
___**Widely** Agreed Upon
___**Not** Applicable

___**Not** Practiced
___**Not Widely** Practiced
___**Somewhat** Practiced
___**Widely** Practiced
___**Not** Applicable

Lisa the pharmacist says,
"Get to know your pastor as a person. Ask him to talk about his non-church interests with you. No one wants to 'talk shop' all the time. Often the best sermon illustrations come from pastors who bring their interest in sports or hobbies to the pulpit. Pastors want to have fun, too, and so encouraging these personal dimensions is a good way of encouraging fun in the congregation. We don't have to be so serious all the time."

Questions for You and Your Church

- What kinds of feedback does the pastor in your church receive? Is the pastor able to receive constructive criticism and learn from it? How can this process be improved?
- A seminary professor observed that the way a church treats its pastor is a sign of the congregation's health—or lack of health. Do you agree or disagree? What signs of health do you see in the way your church cares for its pastor? Do you see signs of ill health?
- Relative to other professions, how much should pastors be paid? Relative to your community, how much should they be paid? Should they be paid comparably to lawyers, nurses, doctors, musicians, accountants, or social workers?
- Does your church have a plan for a sabbatical for your pastor? If not, would the congregation see the benefits of developing one? What obstacles might you foresee?
- Sometimes the plate on the door reads "Pastor's Study." At other churches, it reads "Pastor's Office." The first suggests a place where sustained reading is valued. The second suggests more of an administrator. Regardless of what your pastor's door might say at this moment, do you think the congregation views this room as a study or an office?[14]
- Do you sense a good "fit" between the pastor's personality and unique sense of call and your church? How is it evident (or not)? If there are some conflicts, how might everyone work together to help the pastor's passions and the church's own sense of call strengthen each other?

9

The Pastor's Family
SUPPORTING THOSE WHO SUPPORT THE PASTOR

Christians have many different forms of family—and families change over the course of people's lives. Not every person is called into marriage; not every family wants, or is able to have, children. This chapter speaks very generally of "a pastor's family," and this general language is intended to be inclusive of the many different family situations pastors (and congregants!) have. Indeed, one of the great gifts a congregation can give its pastor is to be welcoming of not only whatever family status a pastor has at the beginning of a pastorate but also family members that may come along through marriage or childbirth.

Long, healthy pastorates are often made possible by good dynamics within the pastor's family. But some pastorates are at risk because of what happens—or fails to happen—in the home. Pastors I spoke with worry about neglecting their families for the sake of the church. (This may be because the pastor overcompensates for struggles in the home by working harder at the office.) And ultimately, tragically, when there are unhealthy family dynamics, the danger of broken marriages and/or sexual misconduct increases dramatically.

In the following expectations, the key words of *boundaries, accountability, maturity, resurrection*, and *eustress* are particularly relevant. With thoughtful cooperation, the *covenant* of marriage and the *covenant* between a church and pastor can strengthen each other. As one pastor's husband noted, "The church has more . . . impact on the internal functioning of the pastor's family than the church usually realizes."[1]

Faithful pastors expect healthy congregations . . .
9.1 – to recognize the peculiar dynamics of "life in the fishbowl."
9.2 – to respect family *boundaries*.
9.3 – to welcome the pastor's family into the church.
9.4 – to give the pastor's family members the freedom to be themselves and to be as active or inactive in the life of the church as they want to be.
9.5 – to recognize that clergy family members are fallible just like everyone else.
9.6 – to give the pastor a choice about living in the manse (if there is a manse).
9.7 – to respect the needs of the family and to involve them in decisions about a manse.

9.1 Faithful pastors expect healthy congregations . . .
to recognize the peculiar dynamics of "life in the fishbowl."

"It's not the whole church usually, but one or two people keeping an eye on your family's behavior is wearying."[2]

—a Lutheran pastor

WHILE THE PASTOR is the one who is *ordained* (set apart), there is a sense that the entire family is also set apart. Some clergy families speak of this as "life in the fishbowl." It feels as if everyone is looking in on the pastor's family to see what they are doing. Although she is appreciative of many aspects of being a clergy spouse, Lisa Konick notes that there is "a darker side, well known to clergy spouses from every religion and denomination, of being the center of so much attention."[3]

What is it like to be in a clergy family, a family in such a fishbowl? Pastors and their families express concerns about many things: unpredictable, emergency interruptions in family schedules; having meetings many nights a week, when children need help with algebra and laundry needs folding; not having true family weekends (taking Friday or Monday off does not create a weekend for families with children in school); and not sitting together as a family during worship, especially important worship services.

The spouses of pastors face particular challenges. A man whose wife is a pastor may feel as if he doesn't truly have a pastor or church home of his own. He may be forced to hear gossip from church members about his spouse, and may feel the church has implicit or explicit expectations of him and his children. Perhaps the church expects the pastoral spouse to take care of young children during worship, so he does not really have a chance to worship. As this last challenge indicates, a pastor's spouse can easily be a solo parent on Sunday mornings.

In addition, there may be other issues. Some spouses are ambivalent about midlife calls to ministry. Chronic low pay for pastors coupled with possibly limited opportunities for spouses easily leads

Ann the young pastor says,
"I remember the 'pounding' my husband and I received from the church. We didn't have much money, and prior to our moving in, the church stocked our kitchen with food of all kinds, including a pound of this and a pound of that. That's the best 'pounding' I ever received!"

Bill the senior pastor says,
"Being a pastor's kid is hard. I was one, and I have two myself. Usually pastors' kids either are model citizens or act out all the time. I won't tell which kind I was! It's not easy when your authority figure at home is also standing up there on Sunday mornings and talking about people doing good things all the time. And everyone in the church wants you to set an example for their kids. But what if you don't want to go to church and don't want to set an example? I was lucky as a pastor: the churches I served when my kids were in the home gave them the space to be themselves."

Lisa the pharmacist says,
"I can only imagine how hard it is for our pastor's wife. He gets invited to this and that, and she ends up with lots of parenting duties. Sometimes, one or two of us in the church will call her up and tell her we'd like to take the kids out bowling or to the movies. We want to support her, too."

to short-term distractions and long-term financial difficulties. If the church does not have adequate staffing (which is the case in many, perhaps most, churches), the pastor's family sometimes serves as uncompensated staff by preparing church mailings, cleaning the church, and doing minor repairs. Families living in manses or parsonages sometimes feel frustrated (or even trapped) by having to live in a home that does not meet the family's needs.

Recognizing these challenges (some of which congregants themselves face in their own lives!), healthy churches welcome the pastor's family, and do wonderful things like helping them move in, bringing vegetables fresh from the farm, and introducing the children to potential playmates.

As with all relationships, the relationship between the church and the pastor's family requires nurturing. Healthy congregations recognize the church's covenantal obligation not just to the pastor, but also to the pastor's family.

At my church, this Expectation is:

__**Not** Discussed	__**Not** Practiced
__**Not Widely** Agreed Upon	__**Not Widely** Practiced
__**Somewhat** Agreed Upon	__**Somewhat** Practiced
__**Widely** Agreed Upon	__**Widely** Practiced
__**Not** Applicable	__**Not** Applicable

9.2 Faithful pastors expect healthy congregations . . .
to respect family boundaries.

"My congregation expects me to be available all the time, 24/7. I can deal with that, but my wife does not like it."[4]

—a Baptist pastor

IN A SURVEY CONDUCTED for this book, over one-third of pastors reported that church "had a negative impact" on life with their families, with almost 10 percent of pastors saying this happened frequently.[5]

Chapter 1 noted that ministry is a vocation that often leads to a lack of *boundaries* between the personal and professional. It's all too easy for pastors to allow their identities to be shaped not by God and their families but by the feelings of the congregation. Chapters 4 and 5 noted that some pastors run the risk of overfunctioning—doing more and more in the life of the church, in part to encourage others but also to meet their own personal needs. Those chapters noted that such behavior by a pastor stifles the congregation because the members often end up underfunctioning. Since the pastor is setting up the coffee and donuts every Sunday, why should congregants volunteer to do that? Pastors who fail to set good *boundaries* thus weaken the congregation. And they can also hurt their own families and themselves. The discussion of the importance of priorities (Expectation 7.2) applies both to the health of churches and to families.

Because the congregation may not understand much about the life of a pastor—her workload, diverse responsibilities, and time commitments—they may never stop to think about what appropriate *boundaries* might be. Indeed, sometimes members of a congregation assume they are paying the pastor to be available twenty-four hours a day. Vacations, too, are subject to the needs of the congregation; if a person is seriously ill, the pastor may be expected to cancel a long-planned family trip.

The failure to develop and adhere to appropriate *boundaries* between the pastor's work and his family life easily leads to a spouse who is perpetually irritated,

Lisa the pharmacist says,
"Sometimes pastors do not like being away from their churches. I've known pastors to feel embarrassed about going away for a few days. I try to tell our pastor that I'm glad he's going away for a few days. I care for him and his family, and I want them to be happy in our church for a long time."

Ed the businessman says,
"Our former pastor believed he had to be at every church meeting, even if he was not really needed. It was ridiculous—sometimes groups couldn't meet because of his schedule. And I can't imagine the toll it took on his family. How do you tell a pastor not to come? We had to assert ourselves and tell him that others could offer the opening prayer."

Dennis the bishop says,
"The pastor needs to be clear with herself, her family, and her congregation about family boundaries. If the pastor indicates that church needs always come first, then church members are more likely to feel comfortable making increasing demands of the pastor. And this means the church and the pastor are ultimately taking advantage of the spouse. It may all be unconscious, but it is not fair. Being clear that, just as for church members, a pastor's first call, a pastor's ultimate priority, is to his or her family is a crucial boundary."

dispirited, or even angry. In such a state, the spouse can hardly be supportive. With pastors working long hours (most pastors say they work a minimum of sixty hours per week), tending to household needs often falls to the spouse. A spouse who prepares a special dinner for his wife may not respond well to her phone call announcing that she cannot be there because of a church "crisis." Children may be at risk as well. There are times when it is crucial for a parent to be with a child (such as when a child is experiencing a significant loss for the first time), but a pastor's job may make this impossible. From a very young age, children can pick up on whether Daddy thinks church people are more important than they are.

Healthy family *boundaries* lead to happier pastors, happier pastoral families, and more effective congregations.

At my church, this Expectation is:

__**Not** Discussed   __**Not** Practiced
__**Not Widely** Agreed Upon   __**Not Widely** Practiced
__**Somewhat** Agreed Upon   __**Somewhat** Practiced
__**Widely** Agreed Upon   __**Widely** Practiced
__**Not** Applicable   __**Not** Applicable

9.3 Faithful pastors expect healthy congregations . . .
to welcome the pastor's family into the church.

"I can always tell the character of a congregation by the way they welcome a pastor's family."[6]

—a denominational executive

IT SEEMS OBVIOUS that a congregation would welcome the pastor's spouse and children just as they would welcome the pastor. But it does not always happen. Lots of things can go wrong.

Most churches are glad that a pastor who is married enters the church accompanied by a spouse who might bring more energy to the community. But a new person, particularly a spouse with the ear of the pastor, can be a threat to the existing ways of doing things (particularly if the congregation has had bad experiences in the past or has people with fragile egos).

Theologically, we are all part of the same body of Christ. But in local practice, there sometimes remains an insider-outsider dynamic that makes it hard for a pastor's spouse and children to feel welcome. Any social group—whether it's a neighborhood association, a tennis club, or a church—can unintentionally make it hard for new people to come in and feel welcome. Without intending to, members of these communities may send signals that what really matters is having had many years together. If you or your family were part of the founding group, you have one status; if you are a newcomer, then you have a different (lower) one. The story goes of the man who moved into a community when he was five and lived there for the next seventy years. At his funeral, the locals were heard to say, "He was almost one of us."

Another danger in the welcoming process is the possibility that some members of the church may not have wanted the new pastor (either because they liked the previous one so much or because they would have preferred another candidate). One or two people who bear a grudge against an incoming pastor can make it difficult for the new family.

In addition, congregations bring their previous experiences with spouses and kids to each new pastoral relationship. A pastor who foisted his wife on a congregation as the new director of the children's

Rita the spiritual director says,
"Like most people, pastors' spouses want to be known and appreciated for who they are, not just for who they are married to. Church members welcome the pastor's spouse by inviting him out for coffee and learning about his own story, his own interests, and his own sense of what he would like from the church. Though a spouse may 'come with' the pastor, the spouse should be cherished as any other prospective member."

Bill the senior pastor says,
"Pastors need to be keen observers of the dynamics of welcoming within a congregation. Do church members feel uncomfortable when outsiders use the education wing? Is there an unstated dress code? If a visitor arrives Sunday morning, do people shake her hand and introduce themselves? Pastors can help the welcoming process for their own families—and for the families of their successors—by guiding the congregation in healthy practices of welcoming."

program may have made it hard for his successors, either because the congregation resented that or because they now expect the pastor's spouse to lead the children's program.

Finally, some congregations have members who are perpetually locked in conflict with whoever the current pastor happens to be. If a congregation does not check these members, their rude behavior toward a pastor's spouse will undermine the pastorate.

Welcoming the pastor's spouse and family goes hand in hand with welcoming new members.

Lisa the pharmacist says,
"We learned the hard way that we had to check the bad behavior of our members. It took a lot of prayer and courage, because these folks were our friends. But we really believed it was inappropriate for church members to talk to the new pastor's wife about how they didn't get anything out of the sermon or go on at length about how great the previous pastor was. People are entitled to their opinions, but they were crossing a line, and we saw a need to step in."

At my church, this Expectation is:

__**Not** Discussed

__**Not Widely** Agreed Upon

__**Somewhat** Agreed Upon

__**Widely** Agreed Upon

__**Not** Applicable

__**Not** Practiced

__**Not Widely** Practiced

__**Somewhat** Practiced

__**Widely** Practiced

__**Not** Applicable

9.4 Faithful pastors expect healthy congregations . . .

to give the pastor's family members the freedom to be themselves and to be as active or inactive in the life of the church as they want to be.

"We need to recognize that spouses may need time to grieve. My wife hated it—hated it— when we moved. We had a church that was great for her before."[7]

—a Lutheran pastor

A CHURCH CALLS A PASTOR—not a spouse to serve as an additional alto in the choir, a child to help fill out the third-grade classroom, or another cook to help with fellowship meals.

That said, many, probably most, pastors' families want to be involved in the life of a church. Healthy churches make it possible for members of the pastor's family to thrive by giving them the space they need either to make a church home for themselves or to be inactive in the church. (This freedom, after all, is what church members want for themselves.) Such congregations are willing to let go of any expectations they might have for the pastor's spouse and children simply as part of their welcoming of the new family.

Most pastors' spouses hope their other halves succeed in a church, and they are willing to help out. (But a spouse who feels forced to do particular jobs can clean up the sanctuary only so many times before resentment builds up like the dust.) Some spouses go to churches reluctantly. They are willing to "go along" with the pastor's personal sense of call, but they remain cautious. A wife may have been pulled from a church she loved, where her children were part of a great youth program and where she had important friendships. Should a new church not give her a grieving process, a time when she can pull back from church activities?

If the pastor's family does not want to be active in the life of a congregation, the church needs to not take this personally. It may or may not be a statement about the members or the quality of the church. A clergy family might not be excited about the community, the home, professional opportunities for the spouse, or the school system. None of these are the church's "fault," but it is easy to see how the church could be "blamed."

Lisa the pharmacist says,

"We'd love to have the pastor's wife join us at our women's Bible study, but we understand if she can't make it or doesn't want to come. Some pastors' wives have been very active in the church (and some members feel that some wives have been too active!). Many of us simply assume she should be just like all the rest, but that's not fair to her. Pastors' spouses and children are like any other Christians, right? Like all of us, they need to listen for God's call for their own lives. And the church needs to respect that."

Bill the senior pastor says,

"My wife and kids have helped me fold bulletins before a Sunday service or rearrange the fellowship hall. Some emergency help comes with the territory. But the church has a primary responsibility for providing adequate staffing and volunteers so the pastor's family is not doing these things on a regular basis. I can tell you from experience that this kind of thing gets old quickly. It's one thing to want to help out; it's quite another to feel like you have to help out."

A clergy spouse treated with respect and given the freedom to be herself will be beneficial to the congregation. She will be active in things that matter to her—and she will not bring resentment to the events and activities in which she chooses to participate.

At my church, this Expectation is:

__**Not** Discussed
__**Not Widely** Agreed Upon
__**Somewhat** Agreed Upon
__**Widely** Agreed Upon
__**Not** Applicable

__**Not** Practiced
__**Not Widely** Practiced
__**Somewhat** Practiced
__**Widely** Practiced
__**Not** Applicable

Dennis the bishop says,
"I advise pastors and their spouses to be clear with each other about their needs, priorities, and preferences for participation in any given church. Once they have agreed that, say, the pastor's husband does not want to be active on a church committee, the pastor can then be clear with the church about how her husband will be involved. It sounds really artificial, but there are so many unstated assumptions in a church. Sometimes you just have to be direct."

9.5 Faithful pastors expect healthy congregations . . .

to recognize that clergy family members are fallible just like everyone else.

"They [church members] expect everything to be fine with my marriage, my kids. If I tell them that I have an urgent need to be with my family, what kinds of looks will I get?"[8]

—an Episcopal priest

THERE ARE A NUMBER of reasons why congregations often have certain expectations for the pastor's family.

Everyone wants a good, healthy family life—and church members often project their own desires on their pastors (see 10.4). Since people often assume that God blesses those who are following God's way, and since (presumably) pastors are doing this, it follows that a pastor's family life should be something of a model. If the pastor is struggling with his marriage, what does that say about his spiritual life?

Indeed, 1 Timothy 3:4–5 makes a well-ordered home life a prerequisite for church leadership. A bishop (or church overseer) "must manage his own household well, keeping his children submissive and respectful in every way—for if someone does not know how to manage his own household, how can he take care of God's church?"

Because the pastor represents order, congregants sometimes look to the pastor to help them keep their own children under control. If the pastor's kids are running around in the sanctuary, doesn't that send a signal that it is perfectly fine to misbehave in church? Under these circumstances, pastors and their families feel a great deal of pressure to keep up appearances.

But pastors' families are human, too. And clergy families are under a great deal of stress—many congregants have no idea how much. The normal things that challenge families—children testing limits, inadequate time give to nurturing the marriage bond, financial strain—are also challenges for clergy families. Indeed, the combination of high stress, pressing time demands, and low compensation can make each of these even more difficult.

Further, clergy spouses and children, like many other people, may not want to be in the fishbowl. A child may be particularly angry about being moved

Rita the spiritual director says,
"There is a distinction between sadness and disappointment, a difference between compassion and judgment. A church in a covenant remembers its responsibility for the pastor and responds to difficulties in the pastor's home by thinking first of the pastor's own distress. Congregants are able to put aside whatever disappointment they might have within themselves and speak with the pastor about problems he is facing with sadness and care for him. Shaped by the compassion of Jesus, they put judgment aside and recognize that God will be at work in any broken situation."

Ed the businessman says,
"Church leaders need to be attentive to the needs of the pastor and her family. This may mean offering their pastor time off with pay so she can help her child struggling with the disease of alcoholism. Healthy churches with good lay leaders can function effectively for quite some time without a pastor, and they need to be prepared to do this. Sure, this takes time and energy, but isn't this what Christians are supposed to do for one another?"

to a new town against his wishes. The constant anger or bitterness of a child can make any home a difficult place. And a congregation should not be surprised—or disappointed—when the pastor's children are not enthusiastic about church activities.

One of the chief needs of many people is a healthy family life. Pastors and churches that face family crises with compassion and mutual support can be a life-saving gift to each other.

Bill the senior pastor says,
"Pastors can set the tone for how the congregation responds to family difficulties. If they keep their own self-righteousness in check and embody grace and compassion, they guide the congregation to do the same for them. If they refrain from thinking of other families as spectator sports, that limits the gossip about all families—including their own. Everyone benefits when the pastor sets a good standard. Sadly, it does not always happen."

At my church, this Expectation is:

___**Not** Discussed

___**Not Widely** Agreed Upon

___**Somewhat** Agreed Upon

___**Widely** Agreed Upon

___**Not** Applicable

___**Not** Practiced

___**Not Widely** Practiced

___**Somewhat** Practiced

___**Widely** Practiced

___**Not** Applicable

9.6 Faithful pastors expect healthy congregations . . .
to give the pastor a choice about living in the manse (if there is a manse).

"Manses are bad for pastors, and therefore they are bad for churches."[9]

—a denominational executive

MANSES, OR PARSONAGES, are residences provided by the church for the pastor. Many churches understand these dwellings as a way of supporting the pastor—and sometimes the homes are quite lovely. Some denominations such as the United Methodist Church provide manses because they move clergy around regularly. Pastors and their families may be asked to move on very short notice from one church to another, so there is a certain logic in having a house available for the incoming pastor. Finally, some churches choose to maintain a manse because this appears to be a more affordable way of supporting a pastor.

When I asked for her thoughts about manses, I was struck by how one denominational executive responded: "Manses are bad for pastors, and therefore they are bad for churches." Recognizing that what may have worked in an earlier era may not work well at all now, she was deeply concerned about the restrictions such housing places on a pastor's ability to take care of her family. In speaking with her and with other pastors, the following problems became apparent.

Not every manse is appropriate for every clergyperson and her family. Manses may well be poorly maintained (like rental properties, the person living in them does not make the decisions about repairs). Pastors who have spent decades in a manse (and who may have been underpaid to begin with) have built up little or no equity; consequently, they have restricted access to retirement homes. Because pastors are living in church-owned property, they are often dependent on the goodwill of the congregation even for simple things like repairs. The pressure to keep the congregation happy (and hence to refrain from asking for money for the manse) restricts the pastor's ability to preach the gospel faithfully. Because a dwelling sometimes seems to be forced on the family without any choice, pastors and their families occasionally report feeling trapped. And churches may also underestimate the drain manses place on church resources.

Ed the businessman says,
"Manses can be beneficial for everyone, but they can also cause financial problems, especially if people are not careful. My cousin's church still has a manse, but it doesn't make much financial sense. The money they keep putting into that thing could have gone to pay a housing allowance for the pastor. And then there are the utilities on an old house with high ceilings! And the last thing you want is the pastor doing repairs on the manse, because his time can be used more effectively. I think they keep putting money into it because they can't imagine the church without the pastor living there."

Ann the young pastor says,
"My husband and I are glad to have a manse. It's a much bigger home than we could have afforded at this stage in our lives. We are able to save some money, and hopefully we will own our own home someday. But we've wondered about whether we can talk with the church about moving out of the manse. They want their pastor to live next to the church, but what if we get to the point that we can buy a house of our own?"

The time that committees and staff spend on manse-related issues could also be used for other purposes.

Although manses remain a vital part of the resources of some congregations, healthy churches are prepared to work with the pastor to explore other possibilities for the pastor's housing.

An approach to a pastor's home grounded in a *covenant* gives the pastor the same choices congregants have for their own homes.

Bill the senior pastor says,
"We lived in a manse once, but it was never really our home. This meant that, in some sense, the church itself was never really our home. Now that's not bad theology—a pastor is called to a church for a season, not forever. And pastors can overstay their effectiveness. But people need to feel at home, and that is true for pastors as well."

At my church, this Expectation is:

__**Not** Discussed
__**Not Widely** Agreed Upon
__**Somewhat** Agreed Upon
__**Widely** Agreed Upon
__**Not** Applicable

__**Not** Practiced
__**Not Widely** Practiced
__**Somewhat** Practiced
__**Widely** Practiced
__**Not** Applicable

9.7 Faithful pastors expect healthy congregations . . .
to respect the needs of the family and to involve them in decisions about a manse.

"The manse was a constant irritant in my pastorate."[10]

—a Baptist pastor

MANY CLERGY WEAR collars as a sign of being yoked to Christ.[11] There is a certain loss of "freedom" that comes with this—but ideally it leads to a greater freedom, the freedom to live out the good news faithfully as a leader in Christ's church. For pastors living in a church-owned manse, there is a similar limitation of freedom that should ideally lead to greater freedom for the gospel. Since the pastor does not have to worry about home maintenance, she will have more time for quiet prayer or recreation with her family.

In practice, it does not always work out that way.

On the one hand, the pastor often has oversight responsibilities for church property. He may end up spending lots of time negotiating repair needs. Between negotiating with both the church and contractors and dealing with his teenage son's wishes for his room, it is easy for the pastor to feel caught in the middle.

On the other, if the laity take too much responsibility for the manse, then the pastor and his family can feel worse. Decisions are made about *their* living space with little regard for their wishes, and the dwelling that should be a sign of welcome, *covenant,* and *safety* becomes instead something else. Because controlling living space is a form of power, having a manse can become one way for a church to exercise power over the pastor.

The point is this: in a *covenant,* church members remember that they are responsible for attending to the needs of the pastor and his family—and this means treating the clergy family as they would want to be treated. At the very least, this entails the church's allowing the pastor and her family to take the lead on decisions regarding the manse.

Churches that maximize the pastor's family's freedom to make the manse their home show trust in their pastors and promote healthy pastorates.

Rita the spiritual director says,
"I work with several pastors who live in manses. Some of them resent the way church members view the manse. Just because the house is the church's property does not mean that congregants should have the right to determine how pictures are hung or how to arrange the flower beds. If church members can let go of their expectations for what the manse should look like, they can make life a lot easier on the pastor. Even though it is the church's property, it is the pastor's home."

Ed the businessman says,
"Pastors need to advocate for the needs of their families, including their housing needs. Most of the pastors I've known are too generous to the church. Pastors know that the $2,000 that could go to fixing the plumbing and making his family more comfortable in the manse could also go to the music program at church. And while a better music program could lead to more members, a pastor's responsibility for his family is a foundation for a healthy pastorate. Having more members seems less important when a marriage is in jeopardy."

At my church, this Expectation is:

___**Not** Discussed
___**Not Widely** Agreed Upon
___**Somewhat** Agreed Upon
___**Widely** Agreed Upon
___**Not** Applicable

___**Not** Practiced
___**Not Widely** Practiced
___**Somewhat** Practiced
___**Widely** Practiced
___**Not** Applicable

Lisa the spiritual director says,
"We feel that the 'committee' in charge of the manse should be the pastor and her family. They should negotiate a budget with the church and have discretion to spend the money as they see fit. Pastors and their families are often under a great deal of stress, and nitpicking about minor repairs or color choices can be very demoralizing. We wanted to avoid all that. There are more important challenges in the life of the church."

Questions for You and Your Church

- Do you think your pastor's family feels like they are living in a fishbowl? Have you had a chance to speak with them about how they feel about their place within the congregation?
- Is your church so busy in the evenings or on weekends that the pastor has little time for family life? If so, what changes could be made to help all the families in the church?
- What kinds of things has your church done to welcome the pastor and his or her family into the church?
- What expectations—stated or unstated—does your church have for your pastor's family? How can you help give the pastor's family the freedom to be themselves in your church?
- If your church owns a manse, would your pastor be able to live elsewhere if he or she were to want to? Why or why not?
- If you have a manse, what are the guidelines for who has responsibility for what and who is authorized to have repairs done?

10

Concluding Expectations
PERSONAL MATURITY AND
COMMUNAL WISDOM

As pastors and laypeople begin to discuss the expectations explored in chapters 3–9, they may find that difficult conversation brings out challenging behavior. Thus this final chapter focuses on shared expectations; each of the expections begins, "Faithful pastors and healthy congregations expect each other . . ."

We are not talking in this chapter about the behavior of persons who are mentally ill. Such people sometimes have less of an impact on the church than those who are simply immature and needy. This chapter addresses the problematic behavior only of the latter, as mental illness falls outside the scope of this book.

Several of the ten principles of chapter 1 are crucial for this chapter. Many pastors recognize that the *eustress* of ministry entails inevitable tensions with congregations, and healthy churches expect the tension that often comes when faithful pastors challenge them. The understandable human need for *safety* remains critical for forthright conversation. And we continue to seek *maturity* so we can conduct ourselves in a way that liberates others to present their better selves. Only then can we practice the *accountability* required of a *covenant* community committed to God's work in the world.

A lay leader once compared a church to a neighborhood association. Unless you do something really wrong, you cannot get kicked out of either. Consequently, these organizations can become places where some people take out their frustrations from work or the home. My hope is that this chapter can help both pastors and congregations recognize and check destructive behavior so that their churches can thrive together in *covenant*.

Faithful pastors and healthy congregations expect each other . . .
10.1 – to anticipate conflict, address differences respectfully, and avoid passive-aggressive behavior.
10.2 – to speak directly and avoid triangulation.
10.3 – to trust that friends will respect honest speech about personal behavior and will be prepared to hold each other accountable.
10.4 – not to idolize or demonize each other or to practice projection.
10.5 – to be close, but not too close—to avoid fusion and codependence.

10.1 Faithful pastors and healthy congregations expect each other ...

to anticipate conflict, address differences respectfully, and avoid passive-aggressive behavior.

"A healthy church would have strong internal procedures for bringing controversies to an end; festering conflict typically feeds the ego needs of only very few people, but has costs for all."[1]

—a Presbyterian layperson

CONFLICT IS INEVITABLE. People disagree all the time—and in churches there can be many natural reasons for disagreement, including mismatches in leadership style or administrative structure, anxiety-producing changes in worship, or simple miscommunication. Sometimes disaffected church members take out their frustrations on others and find ways to turn molehills into mountains. From the pastor's point of view, as we have seen in chapters 3 and 6, when a pastor accepts the *eustress* of servant leadership, he accepts the fact that his calling inevitably involves tension with the congregation—and this tension can be healthy or unhealthy.

Healthy churches have members who trust and respect one another, so the conflicts that inevitably arise remain productive. Members recognize they are sharing in something greater than themselves, so ego needs are less dominant in their disagreements. Because they trust that the Spirit is at work, disagreements are viewed not in terms of who's right and who's wrong, but rather as part of a deliberate discernment process of listening for God's voice. Remembering from the Book of Acts that there has been conflict in the church from the very beginning, these churches realize that "the dynamics that generate differences of opinion are not bad in themselves."[2]

Yet churches often have a very difficult time accepting the fact that there is conflict in the first place. People want comfort and *safety*, which often means we'd rather ignore differences than expose them. Sometimes we cling to the assumption that church is a place where everyone agrees, so we miss signs of simmering frustration or mistrust. Unhealthy conflict—whether it erupts openly or simmers unspoken—can take a toll on the congregation, the pastor, and the pastor's family.

Lisa the pharmacist says,
"I remember a really awkward time in one of our committees. There was one person who kept saying he'd do things, but he never did them. Entire committee meetings were wasted because he did not get the information he said he'd get. After consulting some members of the committee, I offered to call the person regularly before each meeting to check on his progress. I tried to be nice, but he still got testy—no one likes being followed up on. But it was like dealing with a child. I had to keep checking in on him until he had done his 'homework.' But, like a child, he grumbled and eventually did what he needed to do. I don't want to have to do that again."

Rita the spiritual director says,
"Jesus' advice to talk to someone directly when that person has sinned against us is good advice—as long as we are humble enough to admit that we might have sinned against the other person. We all would benefit from meditating on Matthew 18."

Sometimes, when people don't address their conflicts honestly and openly, they resort to passive-aggressive behavior. They don't appear openly hostile; they are not throwing grenades or wadded-up church bulletins. But their failure to show up for a meeting or to complete a task as promised is a passive way of "attacking." Such behavior allows one person to undercut another without making it look intentional or un-Christian.

Such behavior is also hard to correct since there are always apparently valid excuses ("something came up"). Also, there may not be anyone else who can be called upon to handle the tasks the passive-aggressive person has promised to do. Thus, the congregation may feel "stuck" with this person. Passive-aggressive acts undermine the life of the church. Like triangles (see Expectation 10.2), they require that other people pour more time and energy into the church just to get some basic things accomplished. Eventually, people may get so frustrated that they leave or stop participating in the life of the church.

Conflict is inevitable—and can be part of God's work in the community. Pastors and congregants in healthy churches choose to work with God and not against one another.

Ann the young pastor says,
"I remember this one church from when I was teenager. They had a room they could use either for the choir or for a new children's ministry. The members disagreed—disagreed strongly, in fact—and Mom was really worried. But the church members did not 'take sides.' They got through it and made a decision, but they didn't feel like there were winners or losers. They just didn't set it up that way. They handled it well, and I've tried to learn from that."

At my church, this Expectation is:

__**Not** Discussed

__**Not Widely** Agreed Upon

__**Somewhat** Agreed Upon

__**Widely** Agreed Upon

__**Not** Applicable

__**Not** Practiced

__**Not Widely** Practiced

__**Somewhat** Practiced

__**Widely** Practiced

__**Not** Applicable

10.2 Faithful pastors and healthy congregations expect each other . . .

to speak directly and avoid triangulation.

"In the long run, speaking honestly hurts less—as long as we remember to speak the truth in love."[3]

—a Catholic layperson

SOMETIMES SPEAKING with someone face to face is one of the hardest things to do. Some of us are uncomfortable with tension or conflict, so we may not speak up about something that is important to us. Sometimes our desire to please people or keep people happy is so strong that we'd rather internalize a frustration than talk about a problem. Sometimes it has to do with our own sense of *safety* (emotional or even physical). We can get locked into patterns of avoidance, allowing our annoyance to become a kind of simmering anger that makes it hard to interact with the other person in a healthy way.

Instead of speaking directly to the person involved, we may seek out someone else who will talk to the other person. This sometimes is called *triangulation* because it adds a third party to what should be a direct conversation between two people. It can be quite childish—think of the middle schooler who plays one parent off of the other to get what she wants. And people have been known to "invent" third parties. Instead of talking to a church member about his own concerns, a congregant might state, "I've heard people say . . ." As with most forms of immature and needy behavior, triangles take time, drain emotional energy, and foster rumors and incomplete information.

It is easy to "fall" for a triangle. Jim may view his pastor as a hero if she solves his problem with Betty. (Eager to please, many pastors are particularly susceptible to this danger!) But the more heroic stance is for the pastor to encourage Jim and Betty to work things out on their own.

Emotionally mature people in healthy relationships speak directly with each other even about difficult subjects. It is not always easy—tensions can be present, and disagreements may remain unresolved. But such people are able to have respectful conversations. And such people can be helpful in churches by encouraging fellow congregants (and pastors!) to speak to one another directly as well.

Dennis the bishop says,
"Triangles are church killers. Power struggles that arise because of emotional needs—how can they be helpful? Jesus tells us to talk to each other directly when we've got a problem (Matthew 18:15). People who worship the same God in the same place ought to be able to follow that advice."

Bill the senior pastor says,
"It took me forever to figure out why no one would get the committee work done. They didn't like talking with one another, so they avoided one another like the plague. So I'd get calls from a committee member telling me what to tell another member. It was the silliest thing."

Lisa the pharmacist says,
"I guess people trust me or something, since they are always calling me when they are upset at someone else in the congregation. When two people can't speak directly, it takes up lots of time for other people. I am happy to do things for my church, but I don't like it when church members waste my time this way."

Healthy church members trust that respectful conversation about difficult topics is grounded in the work of the Holy Spirit.

At my church, this Expectation is:

__**Not** Discussed	__**Not** Practiced
__**Not Widely** Agreed Upon	__**Not Widely** Practiced
__**Somewhat** Agreed Upon	__**Somewhat** Practiced
__**Widely** Agreed Upon	__**Widely** Practiced
__**Not** Applicable	__**Not** Applicable

10.3 Faithful pastors and healthy congregations expect each other . . .

to trust that friends will respect honest speech about personal behavior and will be prepared to hold each other accountable.

"Good leaders on sports teams stop and talk with teammates about what's going wrong. That's how teams get better. Why doesn't that principle apply to churches?"[4]

—a Lutheran layperson

WE ALL APPRECIATE it when someone else sticks up for us. Pastors and church members are no exception. Pastors are particularly grateful when a church member interrupts the flow of gossip about the pastor's family or tells another church member to stop distorting what the pastor said at a committee meeting.

All too often, however, church members let one another get away with inappropriate behavior. Laypeople and pastors alike have reported stories of snooping in the pastor's office; threatening to withhold a pledge; nickel-and-diming the pastor out of spite; speaking loudly and aggressively in committees; or playing "punch the pastor" (slinging accusations about how the pastor is ruining things).

The Scots Confession, which is part of the Constitution of the Presbyterian Church (USA), identifies three signs of the true church: the "true preaching of the Word of God . . . the right administration of the sacraments . . . and ecclesiastical discipline uprightly administered, as God's Word prescribes, whereby vice is repressed and virtue nourished."[5] The writers of this confession, inspired by Matthew 18:15–35, recognized that irresponsible behavior in a church needed to be addressed if the church would remain the church. It is important to note that one of the stated goals of holding others accountable is nourishing virtue. If we truly love our neighbor—if we truly want the best for him—we don't let him persist in wrong behavior. Rather, we help him do what is right. (Note that Hebrews 12:6 connects God's love with God's discipline.) To be sure, holding friends accountable means risking friendships. As one denominational executive said, "Church discipline is hard, but essential."[6]

Like other volunteer organizations, most churches have few formal mechanisms for checking hurtful

Lisa the pharmacist says,
"It is the responsibility of all of us to promote helpful ways of relating. The pastor is not supposed to be the policeman or truant officer making sure everyone behaves. No, it is my job, too. We let bad behavior go on for a while in our church, and, eventually, everyone paid for it."

Ed the businessman says,
"People get away with things in churches they would never get away with elsewhere. We're such wimps. We appease people way too much. If I'm doing something that hurts someone else, I want people to tell me. I want them to tell me directly. Maybe they don't know the whole story and need to hear me out. Maybe I need to do something differently. A real friend won't be afraid to help me be better."

Ann the young pastor says,
"We've all heard the saying, 'All that is needed for evil to triumph is for good people to do nothing.' That's true in the church, too. I'm a big girl. I can handle it when people have constructive criticism for me. But it really undermines my service if people are sniping behind my back. That's just wrong."

behavior. But healthy churches remain aware of the need for friends to be honest and caring enough to risk uncomfortable conversations about personal behavior. Mature people have no need to be worried about embarrassing discussions regarding who's doing or not doing what. If something wrong is going on, healthy people admit mistakes and ask forgiveness. And Christians are expected to practice forgiveness and go forward.

Churches that practice forgiving and being forgiven are able to promote responsible behavior and to hold themselves to a high standard.

At my church, this Expectation is:

__**Not** Discussed	__**Not** Practiced
__**Not Widely** Agreed Upon	__**Not Widely** Practiced
__**Somewhat** Agreed Upon	__**Somewhat** Practiced
__**Widely** Agreed Upon	__**Widely** Practiced
__**Not** Applicable	__**Not** Applicable

10.4 Faithful pastors and healthy congregations expect each other . . .

not to idolize or demonize each other or to practice projection.

"A pastor should never get more than half the credit when things go right and, unless there has been genuine abuse of power, no more than half the blame when things go wrong."[7]

—a Methodist layperson

MANY PASTORS ARE wonderful people in many different ways. They often embody gentleness, strength, wisdom, and generosity. And churches rightly expect a great deal from their pastors—faith, leadership, training, and integrity. It is easy to see how congregations can put their pastors up on a pedestal and idolize them. The pastor can become the embodiment of what the congregation hopes for itself. Or sometimes the pastor even becomes, in a congregant's imagination, the parent or child he never had or even the idealized self.

Such thinking is unfair to pastors. Unrealistic expectations make it hard for pastors to have their own problems (which, in turn, can lead them to repress those problems in ugly ways). They also can have the unintended consequence of stoking pastoral self-righteousness. A pastor who has become an idol of worship cannot make mistakes and is unlikely to practice forgiveness.

On the other hand, when churches struggle, sometimes pastors get all the blame. Congregations project all their worries and failures onto the pastor. "If only she preached better . . . if only she visited more . . . if only she were more organized. . . . If only." Instead of recognizing the congregants' own responsibilities, this habit of demonizing the pastor stokes the congregation's self-righteousness! Poor administrative structures, lack of spiritual vitality in the members, a sanctuary in disrepair—these are all the pastor's fault, aren't they?

Many pastors recognize these possibilities and appreciate the fact that a congregation's expectations of what a pastor is supposed to be have been shaped by their experiences with previous pastors. It is said that generals are always fighting the previous war. All too often, churches are working with the previous pastor. It is natural that a congregation's expectations of its pastor

Rita the spiritual director says,
"Unfortunately, there is something inside us that needs to project our own hopes or fears, our own desires or guilt, onto other people. We are either looking for a savior or looking for someone to blame."

Bill the senior pastor says,
"The thing I want to get really right in the church is not being the perfect preacher or teacher. I want to get forgiveness right—asking for forgiveness when I make mistakes (and there are plenty!), offering forgiveness when others wrong me, and promoting forgiveness to the entire congregation. I figure the best pastor is the one who can accept the reality of sin without being overcome by it."

Ed the businessman says,
"Are pastors saints? Are they demons? People can assume either extreme, depending on the church and how it is doing. It's easier to see the pastor as the one individual who makes all the difference. But I don't mind telling you that I have enough pride to take responsibility for my actions and for being a part of the success or failure of my church."

are shaped by previous pastors—how wonderful they were as preachers or what problems they had. But healthy churches are careful to recognize that each pastor is different. In chapter 8, we saw that supporting the pastor included respecting her as a unique person and letting her be herself—that is, letting her be the good, but imperfect, pastor she can be. Healthy churches recognize the distinctive gifts and deficiencies of each pastor and accept their own responsibilities for thriving together in *covenant*.

Like most people, pastors appreciate realistic expectations, especially the expectation that they are neither angel nor demon, but rather human.

At my church, this Expectation is:

__**Not** Discussed	__**Not** Practiced
__**Not Widely** Agreed Upon	__**Not Widely** Practiced
__**Somewhat** Agreed Upon	__**Somewhat** Practiced
__**Widely** Agreed Upon	__**Widely** Practiced
__**Not** Applicable	__**Not** Applicable

10.5 Faithful pastors and healthy congregations expect each other...

to be close, but not too close—to avoid fusion and codependence.

"Codependent No More—If That's OK with You"

—slogan printed on a t-shirt

EMOTIONALLY MATURE PEOPLE combine a healthy sense of themselves as individuals with a capacity to be deeply connected to others. They know who they are, what they are responsible for, what they really care about, and what the limits of their interactions should be. They respect their own "I" as a unique person worthy of respect, and they respect "You" as a distinct person, also worthy of respect. Capable of being alone, they also enjoy the company of other people. They can be close without being too close. Some counselors use the term *self-differentiated* to describe such emotional maturity in which a person's own identity is healthy on its own terms.

By contrast, sometimes people are "fused"—too connected to others. A needy person—and let's remember we all have needs!—may have difficulties separating himself from others. He will take things very personally since his sense of worth is grounded too much in what others think of him. At its extreme, he feels responsible for other people's emotions, even when another person's sadness has nothing to do with him.

Sometimes this leads to "codependent" relationships where people lack enough distance and separation to function together in a healthy way. There are few *boundaries*, and people work their way into patterns of controlling others or being compliant with others' needs. Anxiety tends to be high in fused or codependent relationships in part because the relationships are addressing deeply felt emotional needs for *safety*, acceptance, and self-worth. Sadly, codependent people have a sense of fragility.

This dynamic can occur quite frequently in churches. Pastors are notorious for wanting to please people. Chapter 4 noted that a needy pastor can be great detriment to a church (see, for example, Expectation 4.1). Similarly, a needy, fused church can be a detriment to everyone. And congregations can indeed become dependent on the pastor. Pastors and congregations, in other words, can easily go from "close" to "too close." At its worst, the pastor can't imagine how the church could get along

Ann the young pastor says,
"I know they meant well, but when I wanted to go on vacation, two church members said, 'How will we get along without you for two whole weeks?' They said this because they thought I was doing things right—but they made me think about what I must be doing wrong."

Lisa the pharmacist says,
"I like the fact that people trust me and my knowledge of pharmaceuticals. But a big part of my job is making sure they don't actually need me. I'm doing my job well when they leave the store knowing what they need to know. I like the fact that our pastor has the same approach. She teaches us how to pray and read the Bible. She doesn't have to be at every group or committee because we feel ready to do the work of the church. And she respects our freedom to do that."

without her, and the congregation can't imagine how they could ever get along without the pastor. They become codependent on each other and lose sight of the fact that they are really dependent on God.

Paul asks, "Am I now seeking human approval or God's approval? Or am I trying to please people? If I were still pleasing people, I would not be a servant of Christ" (Galatians 1:10). The church person (pastor or congregant!) who is fused or codependent and always trying to please may well no longer be serving Christ or others.

When we try so hard to please others, we have a hard time expressing our own sense of call, and we may also be inhibiting others from taking necessary responsibilities. Further, like a parent who can't bear the thought of a child being unhappy and will give in to the child's demands just to stop her screaming, church folks who feel a pressing need to keep others happy are highly unlikely to set limits on bad behavior.

Healthy churches have less anxiety because their leaders display emotional maturity. They bring respect, humility, and non-anxious trust to both the communion table and the committee table.

Bill the senior pastor says,
"I remember one church where, at first, I thought everyone was just numb. They seemed to lack energy and enthusiasm. It took me a while, but then I realized that they had a lot of energy—but all the energy was going to keeping a lid on the worrying. Everyone knew that certain topics would get a few key people going, and if that happened, everyone would go home upset. They had the hardest time speaking honestly and openly about their own hopes because they didn't want to put a strain on things."

At my church, this Expectation is:

__**Not** Discussed   __**Not** Practiced
__**Not Widely** Agreed Upon   __**Not Widely** Practiced
__**Somewhat** Agreed Upon   __**Somewhat** Practiced
__**Widely** Agreed Upon   __**Widely** Practiced
__**Not** Applicable   __**Not** Applicable

Questions for You and Your Church

- How comfortable are people in your church speaking directly with one another? Are there noticeable exceptions?
- Where are the triangles in your church?
- What inappropriate behaviors have you seen in your church or in other churches? How were they addressed? What did you learn from these incidents?
- What inspiring behaviors have you seen? How might they serve as models?
- What do people expect from their pastor(s)? Are these realistic or fair expectations?
- Are there signs of passive-aggressive behavior in your church? If so, how are people addressing them?
- Do people stake out a position on things in order to get their way? How do others respond?
- What might it mean to be, as one pastor recommended, "power-conscious, but not power-hungry"?
- If you have been in a congregational situation of needing to "speak the truth in love," how did it go? If it went well, what made the difference? If it didn't go well, what can you learn from the experience?

Conclusion
LOOKING AHEAD, WITH SPECIFICS

This book has named a number of expectations for strengthening the *covenant* between congregations and pastors. It may seem like there are too many expectations and way too much to do!

A *covenant*, however, is a living relationship, one that develops over time through steady nurturing. There is no need to address every expectation right away. Indeed, it may be helpful to focus on *the steps that you and your church can take now*. As people have meaningful conversations about how they can best serve God and thrive together, they develop more trust and respect for one another. This strengthening of relationships, in turn, allows for people to enter into more challenging conversations.

As congregations and pastors continue to have such discussions, they can access a wide range of additional resources on topics that were covered only very briefly in this book (as well as issues we've not explored here). The following websites offer good, easily accessible starting points with useful search features:

- Duke Divinity School's Clergy Health Initiative: www.divinity.duke.edu/initiatives-centers/clergy-health-initiative; and Faith and Leadership Program: www.faithandleadership.com
- The Indianapolis Center for Congregations: www.centerforcongregations.org

For now, here are a few questions to get you and the other people in your church going. Space is provided for you to write your answers down. Writing specific responses can be challenging, but such committed action is important. The questions are addressed to both "you" (singular) and "y'all" (plural). While this book is most helpful when read by a group of people in a church community, it may be that at this point you will be responding to questions as an individual. Simple acts by a single person can make a great difference. And in either case, the steps of one person or a group of people may be leavening for the whole.

Specific Steps to Take
- What one step can you take this week to help make a difference in your church?

- What three steps can you take this month to help make a difference in your church?

- What six priorities for the year ahead can you identify to help make a difference in your church?

Specific People to Speak With
- What three people in your church can you speak with about improving the *covenant* between your church and its pastor(s)?

Specific Things to Anticipate
- What three concerns might you have about moving forward with some of the topics raised in this book?

- What three things can you name that lead you to be optimistic about the future of your church and its relationship with its pastor(s)?

Something Specific to Remember

God called your church into being, forming a *covenant* with you, and God continues to be at work in your midst.

Appendix 1
CONDUCTING A MUTUAL MINISTRY REVIEW

In a Mutual Ministry Review (MMR), pastor(s) and lay leaders ask together, "How are *we* doing together in our efforts worship God, guide the congregation, and serve the community?" An MMR is an occasion for giving thanks for what God is doing in the congregation's midst as well as for looking for ways to enhance the life and mission of the church. Typically, the group responsible for overseeing the life of the church conducts the MMR. (Depending on the denomination, this could be the vestry, session, or board of deacons, though sometimes a personnel committee might take on this responsibility; alternatively, this governing board could delegate the work to another group with the expectation of receiving a report for their own deliberation). Prior to the MMR, this group might well ask for input from the entire congregation through interviews, surveys, or sustained conversations.

Good resources for conducting an MMR can be found in a number of places. (Many of the resources below are from Episcopal sources, since this denomination emphasizes MMRs more than most.)

- For a good, succinct general discussion of MMRs, see the Episcopal Diocese of Newark's "Mutual Ministry Review": http://www.dioceseofnewark.org /canon-office/mutual-ministry-review
- For a good overview and several very useful sample forms, see "How to Conduct a Mutual Ministry Review" by Frank Logue, Canon for Congregational Ministries of the Episcopal Diocese of Georgia: http://loosecanon.georgia episcopal.org/?p=402
- For one church's experience, see this narrative provided by St. John in the Wilderness: http://www.stjohnwilderness.org/Voice/bv0602.htm# MutualMinistryReview
- For a very helpful worksheet for setting ministry priorities, see the "Ministry Priorities Worksheet" created by the Florida Conference of the United Methodist Church: http://www.flumc.org/ce/02_ministry_prioritization_work sheet.pdf

This appendix summarizes the advice given in these resources and integrates them with the ten principles for a vibrant church community. After all, a Mutual Ministry Review recognizes the importance of *mutual ministry* and *ordination*, and it promotes *accountability* in fulfilling the church's *purpose*.

An MMR has four major dimensions:

- broad goals
- timing
- specific topics
- process

Broad Goals: What Is an MMR Trying to Do?

In big-picture terms, the goals of an MMR are:

- to help the entire church serve God as faithfully and effectively as possible
- to improve the life and mission of the church
- to strengthen the *covenant* between pastor and congregation
- to help church members live out their own calls to serve

Timing: When an MMR Can Be Helpful

An MMR will be more helpful when a church already has a clear sense of its *purpose*. After all, it is hard to evaluate how things are going when people do not have agreed-upon goals or benchmarks. An MMR is not a substitute for a vision or a mission discernment process wherein a church seeks to discover God's will for the community. An MMR may lead ultimately to a revision of a church's identity, but that is not its primary goal.

For an MMR to be helpful, church leaders need sufficient *safety*. A pastor who is worried about losing his job or a church experiencing conflict will have a hard time assessing strengths and weaknesses honestly. Similarly, an MMR should not be part of the annual review of the pastor's salary. Neither the carrot of increased salary nor the stick of withholding a benefit should interfere with discussion about how the church could function better. An MMR could lead to a new appreciation of the pastor's role and a fresh assessment of appropriate compensation, but these should not be paramount in the minds of church leaders.

Just as *safety* is required, so, too, is *maturity*. A pastor and congregation exhibiting the characteristics of fusion and codependence (or some of the other challenging issues discussed in chapter 10) will be unlikely to have a productive conversation. If there are concerns about the behavior of one or more people in the process, the pastor and lay leaders may need to ask someone from outside of the church to facilitate the discussion. Such a facilitator can set *boundaries* for the discussion that will promote *safety*.

An MMR could be very helpful in the first six months of a pastorate, after enough time has passed for patterns to emerge but before habits are set in stone. Further, MMRs are more useful when congregations embrace them as part of their regular responsibility to everyone in the church. (Thus, some people recommend an MMR every six months.) An MMR should focus on a designated period of time (for example, the last six months or the last year). This discourages going back to old issues in the church's history (unless they still affect the congregation), and encourages concentrating on specific events or practices that are immediately relevant.

It is important to note that churches will conduct MMRs differently. After all, they have different histories, needs, and habits. The important thing to achieve is a thoughtful, open discussion of what is going well and what needs improvement.

Specific Topics: What an MMR Needs to Focus On

Generally speaking, there are two areas of focus for an MMR:

- determining the strengths and weaknesses of the church's current ministry
- clarifying priorities especially for the pastor but also for lay leaders and the congregation

Again, several of the ten principles are significant. As the pastor and lay leaders assess strengths and weaknesses, they may discover the need to practice *resurrection*. They may discern a need for the pastor or members of the congregation to let something die so that something else might live. Note that, as this book has emphasized, reviewing both the distinctive and shared priorities for all members of the church community respects the pastor's *ordination* and strengthens the *covenant* between the one set apart and the community she serves.

Process: How It Works

MMRs need not be complicated. Indeed, less is more, and simpler is more effective. The pastor need not preside at the MMR. If the congregation includes a good facilitator, that person can share her gifts by guiding the meeting.

A good sequence for an MMR would be the following:

1. Discuss the church's *purpose* as a reminder of why the church does what it does. Normally, this *purpose* includes worship, fellowship, support of church

members, and service to the community. A church may have a specific vision of where God is leading it, and/or it may have a mission statement that describes its current activities. Each of these would serve as a useful reference point. As noted above, the goal is not to revise the *purpose*, but to ground the discussion in a shared sense of why the MMR is important.

2. Elaborate strengths of the church's ministry. What are people grateful for? What are people proud of? What is worth sustaining at a high level? Putting these on a whiteboard or flip chart will allow everyone to see all the good things going on.

3. Identify areas for improvement. This can be the hardest phase. Some people may not want to be critical of the preacher (while others may be all too happy to denigrate the preaching). Faithful pastors and healthy congregations, however, have the *maturity* needed to promote the *safety* necessary for honest conversations. In some cases, the nature of the *covenant* between pastor and congregation may need to be discussed. Is the pastor flourishing? Does she need help? Again, a whiteboard or flip chart may be useful for listing areas needing improvement.

4. Develop strategies for addressing issues identified as needing improvement. As stated above, this may involve practicing *resurrection*. It may involve setting better *boundaries*. In this stage, as with the entire MMR, *eustress* may be present. There may be a tension between improving the pastor's administrative work and the necessity of visiting the homebound members of the congregation.

5. As part of the strategizing process, discuss and—ideally—agree upon priorities for the pastor's service. This discussion of the pastor's priorities also involves—in the spirit of genuine *mutual ministry*—a discussion of priorities for lay leaders and other members of the congregation.

6. Finally, agree to plans for implementing changes. These should be specific steps that designated individuals (or groups of people) will take. Also agree when and how to assess if progress has been made.

There may be *eustress* in the process, but, as with regular exercise for the body, hope-filled, purposeful stress brings strength and better health for the body of Christ.

Appendix 2

TEN PRINCIPLES AND FIFTY-SIX EXPECTATIONS FOR A HEALTHY, VIBRANT CONGREGATION

Ten Principles for a Vibrant Church Community
(Chapter 1)

Purpose: Striving to Be the Church
Ordination: Respect for the "Set Apart"
Covenant: A Life-Giving Relationship
Mutual Ministry: We All Serve Together
Resurrection: "Practice Resurrection"
Eustress: Keeping the Inevitable Tensions in Tune
Safety: Don't Take It for Granted
Maturity: Cultivating Honesty, Trust, and Self-Knowledge
Accountability: The Sacrament of Failure
Boundaries: The Difference between Bad and Good, Good and Great

Twenty-Three Expectations for Pastors
(Chapters 3–5)

Healthy congregations expect faithful pastors . . .
3.1 – to understand that ministry is about serving God, not about themselves.
3.2 – to have "pastoral imagination" and to view the church and the congregation theologically.
3.3 – to desire more for their congregations without becoming brokenhearted.
3.4 – to encourage others to have high hopes and to push the church to do its very best.
3.5 – to discern models of ministry relevant to their particular churches.
3.6 – to preach on difficult subjects, even if it makes them unpopular.
3.7 – to lead the people in worshipping the living God.

4.1 – not to take everything personally.
4.2 – to remain calm and to help promote *safety* in the church.
4.3 – to pursue holiness.

4.4 – to be learning and growing constantly.

4.5 – to be involved in a peer group for support, collaboration, and *accountability*.

4.6 – to respect their bodies as temples of the Holy Spirit.

4.7 – to be able to receive care.

4.8 – to honor their own families just as pastors encourage church members to honor theirs.

4.9 – to observe Sabbath rest.

5.1 – to be preparing the congregation for their eventual successors.

5.2 – not to overfunction such that the congregation starts to underfunction.

5.3 – to empower other leaders in the church.

5.4 – to take a sabbatical and let the congregation take a sabbatical too.

5.5 – to honor both silence and speech.

5.6 – to make mistakes, to disappoint, and to practice forgiveness.

5.7 – not to be too proud or insecure to ask for help.

Twenty-Eight Expectations for Congregations (Chapters 6–9)

Faithful pastors expect healthy congregations . . .

6.1 – to serve God above all and, thereby, to meet the people's deepest needs.

6.2 – to be clear about the church's current *purpose.*

6.3 – to believe that churches are called not to survive but to thrive.

6.4 – to trust that money follows mission.

6.5 – to take risks for the sake of the gospel.

6.6 – to recognize that all church members are called to lives of holy service.

6.7 – to let the pastor be a pastor.

7.1 – to establish a clear, realistic job description for the pastor.

7.2 – to work collegially to determine priorities for pastoral ministry.

7.3 – to provide staffing and volunteers adequate for the church's life and mission.

7.4 – to engage in a Mutual Ministry Review for shared *accountability.*

7.5 – to establish a pastor-congregation relations team.

7.6 – to help provide continuing education for lay leaders.

8.1 – to help them see that their *mutual ministry* is making a difference.

8.2 – to pray for the pastor.

8.3 – to provide honest feedback, including both appreciation and constructive criticism.

8.4 – to hold the pastor accountable and practice forgiveness.

8.5 – to provide appropriate financial support.

8.6 – to provide for time off and a regular sabbatical.

8.7 – to value the pastor's time dedicated to prayer and study as an integral part of his service to the church.

8.8 – to give pastors freedom to be themselves and to respect each pastor's unique sense of call.

9.1 – to recognize the peculiar dynamics of "life in the fishbowl."

9.2 – to respect family *boundaries.*

9.3 – to welcome the pastor's family into the church.

9.4 – to give the pastor's family members the freedom to be themselves and to be as active or inactive in the life of the church as they want to be.

9.5 – to recognize that clergy family members are fallible just like everyone else.

9.6 – to give the pastor a choice about living in the manse (if there is a manse).

9.7 – to respect the needs of the family and to involve them in decisions about a manse.

Five Expectations for Everyone
(Chapter 10)

Faithful pastors and healthy congregations expect each other . . .

10.1 – to anticipate conflict, address differences respectfully, and avoid passive-aggressive behavior.

10.2 – to speak directly and avoid triangulation.

10.3 – to trust that friends will respect honest speech about personal behavior and will be prepared to hold each other accountable.

10.4 – not to idolize or demonize each other or to practice projection.

10.5 – to be close, but not too close—to avoid fusion and codependence.

Bibliography

Ammerman, Nancy Tatom. *Congregation and Community.* New Brunswick, NJ: Rutgers University Press, 1997.

Avery, William O., and Beth Ann Gaede. *If This Is the Way the World Works: Science, Congregations, and Leadership.* Herndon, VA: Alban, 2007.

Bailey, Marcia Barnes. *Choosing Partnership, Sharing Ministry.* Herndon, VA: Alban, 1996.

Bass, Dorothy C. *Practicing Our Faith.* San Francisco: Jossey-Bass, 1997.

———. *Receiving the Day: Christians Practices for Opening the Gift of Time.* San Francisco: Jossey-Bass, 2001.

Bass, Dorothy C., and Craig Dykstra. *For Life Abundant: Practical Theology, Theological Education, and Christian Ministry.* Grand Rapids, MI: Eerdmans, 2008.

Frankl, Viktor E. *Man's Search for Meaning.* Boston: Beacon Press, 2006.

Friedman, Edwin H. *Generation To Generation.* New York: Guilford Press, 1985.

Galindo, Israel. *The Hidden Lives of Congregations: Discerning Church Dynamics.* Herndon, VA: Alban, 2004.

Goodman, Denise W. *Congregational Fitness: Healthy Practices for Layfolk.* Herndon, VA: Alban, 2000.

Hauerwas, Stanley, and William H. Willimon. *Resident Aliens: Life in the Christian Colony.* Nashville: Abingdon, 1989.

Ludwig, Glenn E. *In It for the Long Haul: Building Effective Long-Term Pastorates.* Herndon, VA: Alban, 2002.

Mead, Loren B. *The Once and Future Church.* New York: Alban, 1991.

Muller, Wayne. *Sabbath: Restoring the Sacred Rhythm of Rest.* New York: Bantam, 1999.

Neuhaus, Richard John. *Freedom for Ministry.* Grand Rapids, MI: Eerdmans, 1979.

O'Connor, Elizabeth. *Call to Commitment: An Attempt to Embody the Essence of Church.* Washington, DC: Servant Leadership Press, 2009.

———. *Servant Leaders, Servant Structures.* Washington, DC: Potter's House Bookservice, 1998.

Oswald, Roy M. *Clergy Self-Care.* Bethesda, MD: Alban, 1991.

Palmer, Parker. *The Courage to Teach.* San Francisco: Jossey-Bass, 1998.

Parsons, George, and Speed B. Leas. *Understanding Your Congregation as a System.* Herndon, VA: Alban, 1993.

Peterson, Eugene. *The Contemplative Pastor: Returning to the Art of Spiritual Direction.* Grand Rapids, MI: Eerdmans, 1993.

Preston, Gary D. *The Pastor's Soul Series: Character Forged From Conflict.* Minneapolis: Bethany House, 1999.

Purves, Andrew. *The Crucifixion of Ministry.* Downers Grove, IL: InterVarsity, 2007.

Ramey, Robert H., Jr. *You and Your Pastor: Fulfilling God's Mission.* Danville, VA: Ramey, 2011.

Rendle, Gilbert R. *Leading Change in the Congregation: Spiritual and Organizational Tools for Leaders.* Herndon, VA: Alban, 1998.

Richardson, Ronald W. *Creating a Healthier Church.* Minneapolis: Fortress, 1996.

Savage, John. *Listening and Caring Skills: A Guide for Groups and Leaders.* Nashville: Abingdon, 1996.

Schaper, Donna. *Living Well While Doing Good.* New York: Church Publishing, 2007.

Schnase, Robert. *Five Practices of Fruitful Congregations.* Nashville: Abingdon, 2007.

Sellon, Mary K., and Daniel P. Smith. *Practicing Right Relationship: Skills for Deepening Purpose, Finding Fulfillment, and Increasing Effectiveness in Your Congregation.* Herndon, VA: Alban, 2005.

Siler, Mahan. *Anam Cara: Collegial Clergy Communities.* Raleigh, NC: Publications Unlimited, 2008.

Smith, Christian, and Michael O. Emerson. *Passing the Plate.* New York: Oxford University Press, 2008.

Steinke, Peter L. *Healthy Congregations: A Systems Approach.* Herndon, VA: Alban, 1996.

Swinton, John, and Richard Payne, eds. *Living Well and Dying Faithfully: Christian Practices for End-of-Life Care.* Grand Rapids, MI: Eerdmans, 2009.

Taylor, Barbara Brown. *The Preaching Life.* Boston: Cowley, 1993.

Thompson, George B. *How to Get Along With Your Pastor.* Cleveland, OH: Pilgrim, 2006.

Vanier, Jean. *From Brokenness To Community.* Mahwah, NJ: Paulist Press, 1992.

Willimon, William H. *Calling and Character: Virtues of the Ordained Life.* Nashville: Abingdon, 2000.

Notes

Preface

1. This 2008–2009 Pastoral Leadership Grant focused on one of the grant program's four core areas: nurturing well-lived pastoral lives. The final report for this grant was submitted on 9/1/09. This book emerged directly from the research made possible by this grant.

2. Quotations from these focus groups interviews are identified in the endnotes by the focus group number and the page and line numbers of the typescript. For more information on these surveys, see http://divinity.duke.edu/sites/default/files/documents/chi/Overcoming%20the%20Challenges%20 of%20Pastoral%20Work%20preprint%20-%20web%20version.pdf, 5.

Introduction

1. Personal conversation with the author, 4/13/12.

2. Two other very helpful books that aim to help congregations and pastors to flourish together are Robert H. Ramey Jr., *You and Your Pastor: Fulfilling God's Mission* (Danville, VA: Ramey, 2011), and George B. Thompson, *How to Get Along With Your Pastor* (Cleveland, OH: Pilgrim, 2006).

3. Personal conversation with the author, 7/25/09.

4. This pastor who spoke from the heart so movingly was a student in my pastoral care class in July 2011. The students in this class were all active pastors, and we were able to share our joys and frustrations openly. Those who did not have good clergy groups in their own area were particularly grateful for this collegial opportunity.

Part I - Introduction

1. For a discussion of Christians as a hopeful, expectant people, see Richard Payne's "Hope in the Face of Terminal Illness," in John Swinton and Richard Payne, eds., *Living Well and Dying Faithfully: Christian Practices for End-of-Life Care* (Grand Rapids, MI: Eerdmans, 2009), 205–225.

Chapter 1

1. Viktor E. Frankl, *Man's Search For Meaning* (Boston: Beacon Press, 2006).

2. *Book of Order, The Constitution of the Presbyterian Church (USA)*, Part II (2011/2013), F-1.0304 and F-1.0301.

3. See Robert H. Ramey Jr., *You and Your Pastor: Fulfilling God's Mission* (Danville, VA: Ramey, 2011).

4. Her observations agree with the discussion of the lifespan of churches in Israel Galindo's *The Hidden Lives of Congregations: Discerning Church Dynamics* (Herndon, VA: Alban, 2004).

5. Richard John Neuhaus, *Freedom for Ministry* (Grand Rapids, MI: Eerdmans, 1979).

6. Personal conversation with the author, 11/25/09. The speaker here was a second-career pastor who had been used to having clear job descriptions in his first vocation.

7. Wendell Berry, "Manifesto: The Mad Farmer Liberation Front," from *The Country of Marriage* (New York: Harcourt Brace Jovanovich, 1973), http://www.poemhunter.com/poem/manifesto-the-mad-farmer-liberation-front/.

8. Selye's works include *The Stress of Life* (New York: McGraw-Hill, 1956) and *Stress without Distress* (Philadelphia: Lippincott, 1974).

9. See their *Managing Polarities in Congregations: Eight Keys for Thriving Faith Communities* (Herndon, VA: Alban, 2009).

10. For more information on Therese Schroeder-Sheker and her work, see www.chaliceofrepose .org or her *Transitus: A Blessed Death in the Modern World* (Mt. Angel, OR: St. Dunstan's Press, 2001).

11. Personal conversation with the author, 3/21/08.

12. *The Book of Confessions, The Constitution of the Presbyterian Church (USA)*, Part I, "The Scots Confession," 3.18.

13. This is one of the important teachings in Schroeder-Sheker's music-thanatology program. For more on this program, see www.chaliceofrepose.org.

14. Personal conversation with the author, 10/21/09.

15. For published research from Duke Divinity School's Clergy Health Initiative, see http://divinity.duke.edu/initiatives-centers/clergy-health-initiative/what-we%E2%80%99re-learning/published-research-0. For a summary of stresses facing clergy, many of which relate to the lack of boundaries in the professional as well as citations on further research, see http://divinity.duke .edu/sites/default/files/documents/chi/Overcoming%20the%20Challenges%20of%20Pastoral%20 Work%20preprint%20-%20web%20version.pdf, 2–3. According to the CHI website, "This is the pre-peer reviewed version of the following article: Miles, A., & Proeschold-Bell, R.J., (2012). Overcoming the Challenges of Pastoral Work?: Peer Support Groups and Mental Distress Among United Methodist Church Clergy. Sociology of Religion: A Quarterly Review, which has been published in final form at http://socrel.oxfordjournals.org/content/early/2012/11/01/socrel.srs055."

16. Personal email to the author, 1/21/09. The person who corresponded with me on this project has developed a professional practice of providing counseling to pastors. Both pastors and their churches benefit from such service.

Part II - Introduction

1. Personal conversation with the author, 7/19/09. This quotation is a paraphrase; the conversation came about after I bumped into a friend in the supermarket, and I did not have pencil and paper handy. I have enjoyed these kinds of unexpected conversations, and the people who spoke with me in such unofficial moments seemed to appreciate the opportunity to speak openly about life in the church.

2. Barbara Brown Taylor, *The Preaching Life* (Cambridge, MA: Cowley, 1993).

Chapter 3

1. Andrew Purves, *The Crucifixion of Ministry* (Downers Grove, IL: InterVarsity Press, 2007), 9.

2. Purves, *Crucifixion*, 11, emphasis in the original.

3. Craig Dykstra, "Pastoral and Ecclesial Imagination," in D.C. Bass and C. Dykstra, editors, *For Life Abundant: Practical Theology, Theological Education, and Christian Ministry* (Grand Rapids, MI: Eerdmans, 2008), 5–51.

4. See Dykstra, "Pastoral."

5. George B. Thompson, *How to Get Along with Your Pastor: Creating Partnership for Doing Ministry* (Cleveland, OH: Pilgrim, 2006), 112.

6. Interview with the author, 2/16/09.

7. This is a paraphrase of a personal conversation with the author, 10/7/09.

8. This quotation has been the regular saying of a dear colleague.

9. Interview with the author, 4/18/10.

Chapter 4

1. This description of wisdom is derived from Ronald W. Richardson, *Creating a Healthier Church: Family Systems Theory, Leadership, and Congregational Life* (Minneapolis: Fortress Press, 1996), 85.

2. Parker J. Palmer, *Let Your Life Speak: Listening for the Voice of Vocation* (San Francisco: Jossey-Bass, 2000), 49–50.

3. Mahan Siler, *Anam Cara: Collegial Clergy Communities* (Raleigh, NC: Publications Unlimited, 2008), 23.

4. Richardson, *Creating*, 81.

5. For a good discussion of these terms with particular reference to the life of churches, see Richardson's *Creating*.

6. Richardson, *Creating*, 81.

7. Interview with the author, 6/23/09.

8. Personal conversation with the author, 4/11/10.

9. Personal conversation with the author, 12/18/09. The context for this conversation was listening to Brahms' Requiem and the difference it can make for pastoral ministry.

10. For more on this evocative phrase, see Jean Leclercq's classic study, *The Love of Learning and the Desire for God: A Study of Monastic Culture* (New York: Fordham University Press, 1982).

11. Siler, *Anam*, 23.

12. Siler, *Anam*, 1–2.

13. Parker Palmer, *The Courage to Teach* (San Francisco: Jossey-Bass, 1998), 144.

14. Siler, *Anam*, 8.

15. Clergy Health Initiative focus group interview (2008), FG 1, p. 6, line 27.

16. For more information on the Clergy Health Initiative, see http://divinity.duke.edu/initiatives-centers/clergy-health-initiative.

17. Andrew Purves, *The Crucifixion of Ministry* (Downers Grove, IL: InterVarsity Press, 2007), 16.

18. Interview with the author, 7/2/10.

19. Clergy Health Initiative focus group interview (2008), FG 1, p. 36, line 31.

20. Dorothy C. Bass, "Keeping Sabbath," in Bass, ed., *Practicing Our Faith* (San Francisco: Jossey-Bass, 1997).

21. Author's survey, 4/24/2009. By agreement with the judicatory, the group of clergy surveyed here remains anonymous.

22. Bass, *Practicing*, 88.

Chapter 5

1. For a good online resource on servant-leadership, see www.servantleadershipmodels.com.

2. Personal conversation with the author (paraphrase), 5/7/08.

3. Interview with the author, 11/23/09.

4. Interview with the author, 1/17/08.

5. Interview with the author, 7/2/10.

6. Personal conversation with the author, 4/3/10.

7. Interview with the author (paraphrase), 12/4/09.

8. Interview with the author, 6/23/09.

Chapter 6

1. John Richardson, sermon on the occasion of the installation of Rev. Valerie Melvin to the First Christian Church (Disciples of Christ), Reidsville, NC, May 1, 2010.

2. Author's survey, 12/15/08.

3. Elizabeth I. Steele, "How Responding to People's Needs Hurts the Church," *Congregations*, Spring 2008.

4. Augustine, translated by Albert C. Outler, *Confessions*, I.I. This translation is available online through the Christian Classics Ethereal Library at http://www.ccel.org/ccel/augustine/confessions .pdf. This is a very useful online resource for important Christian texts.

5. Interview with the author, 11/5/09.

6. Interview with the author, 2/21/09.

7. Israel Galindo, *The Hidden Lives of Congregations: Discerning Church Dynamics* (Herndon, VA: Alban, 2004), 57–76.

8. George B. Thompson, *How to Get Along With Your Pastor* (Cleveland, OH: Pilgrim, 2006), 107.

9. Personal conversation with the author, 5/26/09.

10. Interview with the author, 4/18/10.

11. Interview with the author, 6/23/09.

12. Interview with the author, 11/05/09.

13. Interview with the author, 1/14/09.

14. Interview with the author, 11/23/09.

15. Interview with the author, 11/23/09.

Chapter 7

1. Personal conversation with the author (paraphrase), 11/25/09.

2. The layperson who spoke these words to his pastor over the phone was relaying his conversation at a monthly meeting of laypeople and clergy in 2009.

3. Interview with the author, 8/3/09.

4. See http://www.acswebnetworks.com/episcopaldiocesofsv/article290867.htm.

5. The very useful advice "Don't Panic" appears on the cover of Douglas Adams's *The Hitchhiker's Guide to the Galaxy*, a guide for galactic travelers. Was this inspired by Jesus' frequent statement, "Do not be afraid"?

6. See his DVD, *Why You Should Develop a Pastor-Parish Relations Committee* (Herndon, VA: Alban, 1994).

7. Personal conversation with the author, 2/8/2008. My conversation with this pastor was part of our preparation for a training for laypeople and clergy. This pastor was extraordinarily passionate about equipping laypeople.

Chapter 8

1. The first of these quotations came from an interview with the author, 4/18/10. The story about churches doing a previous pastor wrong was a familiar anecdote at a church where I once served. The final of these three introductory quotations comes from a survey by the author, 2/19/10.

2. Interview with the author, 7/21/12.

3. Personal conversation with the author, 7/19/09.

4. Eugene Peterson, *The Contemplative Pastor: Returning to the Art of Spiritual Direction* (Grand Rapids, MI: Eerdmans, 1993), 89.

5. Interview with the author, 11/05/09.

6. Interview with the author, 7/2/10.

7. This is a paraphrase from a statement made by one of the respondents to a Clergy Health Initiative focus group interview (2008), FG1, p. 29, line 24.

8. See "Hero Pilot: Airlines in Shambles," CNNMoney.com, 2/24/2009.

9. For a very useful assessment of patterns of congregational giving, see Christian Smith and Michael O. Emerson, *Passing the Plate* (New York: Oxford University Press, 2008).

10. This comment is reported to me in a personal email from another Presbyterian lay leader, 9/2/09.

11. Interview with the author, 12/14/08.

12. Andrew Purves, *The Crucifixion of Ministry* (Downers Grove, IL: InterVarsity Press, 2007), 126.

13. Interview with the author, 5/2/09.

14. In his classes on pastoral ministry, William H. Willimon lamented the shift he had seen in his own lifetime from having a pastor's study to having an office.

Chapter 9

1. Undated manuscript sent to the author following email exchanges in November and December 2010, 2.

2. Interview with the author, 2/20/09.

3. Lisa Konick, "Life in the Holy Fishbowl: The Challenges and Joys of Being a Clergy Spouse," http://www.beliefnet.com/Love-Family/2000/03/Life-In-The-Holy-Fishbowl.aspx.

4. Interview with the author, 10/6/09.

5. Author's survey, 4/24/09.

6. Interview with the author, 11/18/08.

7. Interview with the author, 5/7/08.

8. Interview with the author (paraphrase), 7/12/09.

9. Phone conversation with the author, 4/23/08.

10. Interview with the author, 7/2/10.

11. The theme of being bound in order to be freed for the gospel is an important topic in Richard John Neuhaus, *Freedom for Ministry* (Grand Rapids, MI: Eerdmans, 1979).

Chapter 10

1. Conversation with the author, 11/14/2010.

2. George B. Thompson, *How to Get Along With Your Pastor* (Cleveland, OH: Pilgrim, 2006), 104.

3. Interview with the author, 9/24/11.

4. Interview with the author, 1/24/2009.

5. *The Book of Confessions, The Constitution of the Presbyterian Church (USA)*, Part I, "The Scots Confession," 3.18.

6. Interview with the author, 11/18/08.

7. Interview with the author, 7/06/09.

CPSIA information can be obtained at www.ICGtesting.com
Printed in the USA
BVOW10s1532090614

355847BV00002B/2/P